BALANCE OF PAYMENTS

Des sciences physiques aux sciences morales (Introduction à l'étude de la morale et de l'économie politique rationnelles). Alcan, 1922. Translated into English by Oxford University Press and Johns Hopkins University Press.

Sur une théorie de l'inflation. Berger-Levrault, 1925. Out of print.

Théorie des phénomènes monétaires. Statique. Payot, Paris, 1927. Out of print.

Une erreur économique: L'organisation des transferts. Doin, 1929. Out of print.

La crise du capitalisme. Editions de la *Revue Bleue,* 1925. Out of print.

L'ordre social. 3rd ed., Librairie Médicis, 1967. Translated into German and Spanish.

Epître aux dirigistes. Gallimard, 1949. Translated into English and Italian.

La régulation monétaire et le problème institutionnel de la monnaie. Recueil Sirey, 1953. Translated into English.

Discours sur le crédit. Edition du Collège Libre des Sciences Sociales et Economiques, 184, Boulevard Saint-Germain, Paris 6e, 1961.

L'âge de l'inflation. 4e Edition, Payot, 1964. Translated into English, Spanish, and Italian.

BALANCE
OF PAYMENTS

PROPOSALS FOR THE RESOLUTION OF

THE MOST PRESSING WORLD ECONOMIC

PROBLEM OF OUR TIME

by Jacques Rueff

Member of l'Académie française and

l'Académie des sciences morales et politiques

Translated by Jean Clément

The Macmillan Company   NEW YORK

To the young research workers who will replace us,

In the hope that they can successfully convince

governments and administrative authorities that balance-

of-payments matters are serious matters

CONTENTS

PREFACE

Since 1958 the federal government has been making the same solemn statement at the beginning of the year, saying that our balance-of-payments deficit will be eliminated before long, and year after year the problem is still with us.

What is the explanation for this persisting failure?

In this timely and invaluable book, Jacques Rueff provides a clear, scientific answer based on facts and examples that can be verified.

Jacques Rueff says we are putting the cart before the horse. It is vital to balance the United States foreign accounts, says Rueff, but our main and urgent problem is to restore an efficient system of international payments, one that will see to it that deficits or surpluses of the balance of payments of individual countries are promptly corrected. Such a system implies that the debtor countries lose what the creditor countries gain. The international gold standard is an outstanding example.

Unfortunately our experts in the government were, and apparently still are, convinced that the deficit of the United States balance of payments can be corrected by administrative, bureaucratic means that try to reduce our expenditures abroad. Hence measures like the equalization tax on the purchase of foreign investments by United States citizens. We are being told that our troubles are caused by capital movements, war expenses, or foreign aid.

For many years Jacques Reuff has taken issue with our experts' methods in attempting to balance our foreign accounts. He keeps arguing that there is no example of an administrative approach to the problem of eradicating a country's deficits in the balance of payments that has brought satisfactory results.

Basing his assertions on solid fact, Rueff demonstrates that it is the function of the balance of trade and services to balance the capital movements of a country, and not the reverse.

Why then are the United States surpluses of trade and services insufficient to offset the deficits of the capital balance? Rueff proves that the gold exchange standard is responsible for this deficiency.

Students of monetary problems will read with interest Rueff's views on the formation of prices and the chapter on the regulation of money supply. Keynes asserted that the quantity of money is not determined by the public. Rueff contends that the public exercises a great influence on the quantity of money in circulation by determining individually the cash balance wanted. He asserts that the central problem of the monetary policy of a country is to maintain, continuously, the money supply at the level of the total amount of cash balances desired by the public.

It is to be hoped that our experts, members of our government and of our Congress, bankers, and academicians will read this book for the good of our country and of the Western World.

PHILIP CORTNEY
Former Chairman
U.S. Council of the International
Chamber of Commerce

INTRODUCTION

It is strangely paradoxical that the governments of France and the United States, which hold opposing views concerning the desirability of an international monetary conference, should be in agreement on a fundamental point of doctrine—that the elimination of the United States balance-of-payments deficit must necessarily precede any modification of the international monetary system.[1]

Indeed, following the Washington talks between the Chancellor of the Exchequer and the Secretary of the Treasury, the United States Government published the following communiqué on June 30, 1965: "In the present circumstances, the primary contribution that the United Kingdom and the United States can make to world financial stability and the improvement of the world monetary system is to achieve and sustain a broad equilibrium in their international balance of payments."

The French Minister of Finance and Economic Affairs, for his part, handed the following statement to the press on July 19, 1965: "The procedure suggested (by the United States Secretary of the Treasury) which consists in convening

[1] The balance of payments of a "currency area" in a given period is the difference, on the plus or minus side, between total payments effected from abroad (i.e., by means of purchases of domestic currency in exchange for foreign currencies or gold) and payments effected abroad (i.e., by purchases of foreign exchange or gold against the domestic currency), excluding transfers relating to settlement operations not arising out of exchange or financial transactions.

The term "currency area" refers to any area integrating all those economic activities which give rise to *de jure* or *de facto* settlements in the currency characteristic of the area concerned.

an international monetary conference does not seem to him a timely proposal. Two conditions must be met first: Before a new monetary system can be established, it is essential to place the existing one on a sounder basis. No doubt, some progress has been made towards equilibrium by those countries which have been suffering from considerably and lasting balance-of-payments deficit. One must still make sure that the recovery is of a durable nature . . ."

The common attitude of the two governments is naturally based on the implicit belief that the smooth operation and durability of an international monetary system require that the balance of payments of participating countries be in equilibrium, whereas I am convinced that an efficient international monetary system alone can secure lasting equilibrium for such balances of payments.

That is where the problem of the chicken and the egg lies.

It is essential that the problem be completely and promptly resolved.

Now, if the governments of the United States and France are right, all those policies which in the past were intended to restore balance-of-payments equilibrium by means of administrative or authoritative action are justified.

Mercantilism, which characterized the trade policy of Europe for centuries, quotas and exchange controls that blossomed forth after the Great Depression, the theory of the "structural dollar scarcity" that brought about the renouncement of Europe during the years which followed the Second World War—all seem fully justified.

Furthermore, the attempts by the United States government to restore balance-of-payments equilibrium over the past four years by reducing its expenditure and the expenditure of its nationals abroad are legitimate.

If, on the contrary, my views are correct, then such policies are unfounded and the efforts tending to restore equilibrium in the United States external settlements without altering the monetary system are doomed to failure.

This book is devoted to a clarification of this very serious problem.

The issue that it attempts to resolve is a simple one: In present circumstances, with the degree of rigidity—in particular employers' and workers' unionization—that characterizes the Western economies, are balances of payments the resultant of the discretionary behavior of all the parties, whether public or private, that contribute to their formation, or are they dictated, as one used to be taught, by efficient monetary influences?

The problem is not only one of economic theory. The answer will have a decisive influence on economic policy because it will directly affect the modalities, and therefore the magnitude, of international trade and even human relations between residents in different currency areas. It will therefore have broad repercussions on the standard of living and the living conditions of the people concerned.

It is this question, as expressed above, that has determined the structure of the present book.

Part one presents mostly facts. A physicist who sets forth a correlation never maintains that it is correct or incorrect in absolute terms. He merely records the degree of precision with which, in specific circumstances, it governs the phenomena observed.

I have attempted to follow the same method and have gathered together in the first three chapters studies devoted to recent situations that raised the balance-of-payments problem.

Chapter 1 is a very general exposé of the present situation of the vexing balance-of-payments problem, as it arises in particular in connection with the United States external deficit.

Chapters 2 and 3 reproduce studies which have been published before: the first which relates to the dollar scarcity problem, in 1949, the second which deals with the problem of German reparations, in 1929.

A scientific theory is considered correct only if it makes forecasting possible. It is in order to submit to the test of the same criterion the theory on which my earlier attitudes were based that I have systematically refrained from altering anything in the text of these earlier publications.

This scruple has one disadvantage: I have had to be over-repetitious, because on several occasions, in order to demonstrate the same principle, I had to adduce the same arguments all over again. I have reconciled myself to this disgrace in order to avoid ever having to isolate the expression of an opinion from the evidence on which it was based.

Part two of this book is devoted to an outline of a theory of international trade.

My theory differs from the classical theory, which, while it explains the facts of equilibrium, does not account for the fact that balance-of-payments deficits are always bound up with the development of processes of prolonged inflation.

It does not account either for the unquestionable, although limited, influence which discount or open-market policies have on the net result of balances of payments.

Lastly, the classical theories are obviously not sufficiently subtle for interpreting the precise facts of equilibrium that have been gathered in the first part of this book.

Indeed, it is my feeling that it is precisely the imperfection of theory—particularly in the monetary field—that accounts for the fact that economists have been denying the facts of equilibrium, however incontrovertible, to which I have never ceased calling their attention.

In an attempt to convince them, I have brought together in the second part of the book two purely theoretical studies that really deal with the same problem—the mechanism of monetary regulation—but in two very different forms. The one: "Influences Regulating the Amount of Currency and the Institutional Problem of Money," published in 1953, was intended to provide the detailed statement of a strict explanation, for which I had been feeling the need since the publication of "L'Ordre social" ("Social Order"), but which I had never expounded in a comprehensive way. It was intended to convince me, more than the reader, of the validity of an analysis that deviated substantially from traditional avenues of thought and prevailing opinion.

As several colleagues told me that they had had real difficulty in following the alchemy of a very abstract piece of reasoning, the second article, entitled "Elements for a Theory of the Discount Rate and the Balance of Payments" incorporated a simpler and, I hope, more readable exposition of the same theory.

I must confess that up until now my theory—whose tenets (at the risk of being taxed with lacking modesty) I hold incontrovertible—has not met with the degree of concurrence that would make it an effective instrument for action. Before it could claim to take the place of classical theory, it must undergo the test of discussion and benefit from a process of collective elaboration that alone can improve its formulation.

It is strange that in an era when so much time and money are devoted to scientific research, a problem that has been dominating the international political scene and whose solution directly affects the welfare and security of all the peoples of the world should have been explored so little and always by means of methods so utterly lacking in precision.

If this book were to give rise to such econometric research and theoretical reflections as would make it possible to confirm or invalidate the theory which to me seems the true one, it would have entirely fulfilled its purpose.

I dedicate it to young researchers, in the hope that they will find in it reasons for doing better than we have and the means of placing at the disposal of governments the possibilities for reasoned and effective action that at present are so direly lacking.

BALANCE OF PAYMENTS

PART ONE

THE FACTS BENEATH

THE PROBLEM

1

THE PROBLEM OF THE 1960'S, FOCUSING ON THE UNITED STATES BALANCE-OF-PAYMENTS DEFICIT[1]

The date when this was first written accounts for the importance attributed to the views of Mr. Robert Roosa, the then Undersecretary to the Treasury of the United States, who represented his Government on the various Committees that had been entrusted by the OECD or the Group of Ten with the task of resolving the monetary problem. Although he has now been replaced in his functions by Mr. Deming, the doctrine he advocated and expounded with particular clarity in the *Foreign Affairs* article mentioned below remains as important as ever because it still represents the views of the United States Government. It is for that reason that, notwithstanding the retirement of Mr. Roosa, the 1963 comments are still topical and have been reproduced in full in this chapter.

[1] This chapter was written in November 1963, on the occasion of a statement—hitherto unpublished—to the annual meeting of the "Collège Libre des Sciences Sociales." Since then, the text has been updated and extended appreciably.

3

For the past fifty years, balance-of-payments matters have caused constant agitation on the political scene.

Those who lived through the first postwar period have not forgotten the storms aroused by the quarrel over German reparations.

Immediately afterward, the Great Depression of the years 1931–33 made many countries insolvent in their foreign relations, causing suspensions of payments in pursuance of international obligations, import quotas, exchange controls, and clearing agreements to become widespread throughout the world, with the result that there was considerable whittling down of international trade everywhere.

After the last war, the "dollar scarcity" caused havoc throughout Europe. It had gradually depleted the French foreign currency reserves and had compelled France, early in 1958, to re-establish import quotas and strict control of all its international transactions, notwithstanding existing commitments.

Today, it is the reverse situation that poses very serious problems for the whole of the Western world. The situation is characterized by an extreme oversupply of dollars outside the United States as a consequence of the prolonged deficit of the United States balance of payments. The present study concentrates primarily on this situation.

The importance to the world of the United States balance of payments

The importance of the United States balance-of-payments problem is proved by the fact that the late President Kennedy, with the clarity and frankness characteristic of his brilliance, devoted one of his first speeches to this topic shortly after his installation in the White House, on February 6, 1961.

He pointed out that between January 1, 1951 and December 31, 1960 the total United States foreign payments deficit amounted to 18,100 million dollars.

In 1961, 1962, 1963, and 1964, respectively, it was 3,000, 3,600, 3,200, and 3,000 million dollars.

As a result of these deficits, the United States gold stock fell from about 23,000 million dollars at the beginning of 1958 to 15,500 million at the end of 1964, while foreign short-term claims against that gold rose from 15,000 million to 28,000 million dollars.

Clearly, if the present trend were to continue, it would inevitably raise difficult problems.

In France, we are thoroughly familiar with this situation and the inescapable character of its consequences.

After the war, our balance of payments showed a very large deficit. From the beginning of 1958, we were moving toward a state of near-bankruptcy, which we practically reached in June 1, 1958. At that date, we had about six weeks' foreign currency left. We were certain that, unless the situation were rapidly restored, we should be obliged to reduce greatly our imports, even of raw materials, thus accepting the paralysis of the factories that used them and the unemployment that would be the painful consequence.

To measure the imperative character of the consequences of a balance-of-payments deficit, it is enough to recall that France had been compelled, notwithstanding the solemn character of the international commitments it had undertaken, to decide, on June 18, 1957, to reintroduce import quotas and, later, to extend this backward-moving procedure to all the items in the customs tariff.

There can be no doubt that if the United States balance of payments were to remain as it is, the United States would be led, whether it liked it or not, to seek similar solutions.

Naturally, the introduction of import quotas in the United States would involve identical measures in Europe, which would inevitably extend to intra-European trade.

Any such happenings would do away with all the progress made during the last two decades in the liberalization of trade, would be an obstacle to Atlantic unity, and would deal a blow, probably fatal, to the European Community.

But even before any such consequences came about, the challenge to the standing of the dollar and the expectation of the measures that would be necessary to protect it would gravely threaten the welcome currency convertibility that had been restored in the West early in 1959. The expansion of international trade and the steady rise in standards of living that had been the consequence would have been jeopardized beyond repair.

But there is another reason that makes us all dependent on the stability of the dollar, namely that at the beginning of 1959 the rates of nearly all convertible currencies were pegged to the dollar and that a large part of the assets that back most of them consists of indebtedness in terms of dollars. Any challenge to the free external convertibility of the dollar would profoundly shake the financial order that has been so painfully restored and would take the West back, probably for a long time, to the monetary disorders from which it had finally emerged.

For all these reasons, a Frenchman cannot be said to be interfering in something that is none of his business if today he ponders over the problem raised by the alarming condition of the United States balance of payments. It is our duty, as well as our right, to look into those facts concerning it.

The position of the United States Government

The dangers which have just been outlined have certainly not escaped the notice of the monetary authorities, particularly those in the United States. On several occasions, and especially since 1961, they have declared their firm intention of countering them. With a rare objectivity, they have sought a common study of the international aspects of their monetary situation. A special committee, known as Working Party

No. 3, has in fact been set up for this very purpose at the OECD, and in September 1963 the International Monetary Fund set up two Committees with the task of proposing workable solutions within a year.

The leading statement of an attitude toward these problems comes from my friend Robert Roosa, the very distinguished and learned Assistant Secretary to the United States Treasury. His point of view has been expressed with the clarity that distinguishes all his utterances in the October issue of *Foreign Affairs* under the suggestive title, "Reforming the International Monetary System."

This title decisively marks the fact that it is indeed a program of reform which Robert Roosa proposes, and we are justified in assuming, because of the post he holds, that this program is also that of the United States Government.

The object of the present study is to throw light on the principles underlying American policy and to weigh its chances of success in the light of the consequences it is likely to have for the whole of the West.

In Robert Roosa's view, the major monetary problem is that of international liquidity. He is afraid that it will not grow fast enough during the next few years and he would like attention to be paid to ways and means of increasing it.[1]

He nevertheless fears that the large United States balance-of-payments deficit may be an obstacle to the objective examination by Governments of this long-term problem. He says:

> That deficit has, to be sure, been the major cause of imbalance in the international payments system for nearly six years. But the President's program, presented on July 18, 1963, demonstrates emphatically the determination of the United States to correct its own deficit, and to keep a sharp separation between that effort and any inter-governmental review of the prospects and arrangements for international liquidity in the future.

[1] This view is still held today by the United States Government as well as by the Governments of the Group of Ten, which asked the Ossola Committee to prepare a report on the creation of reserve instruments.

This stand is so important to the author that he confirms it four times in the course of the article: "That is why it is not possible under the pretext of any new kind of approach to international liquidity to escape the real necessity for balancing the United States' own accounts, as soon as that can practicably be done."

"The United States must, of course, re-establish balance-of-payments equilibrium to maintain confidence in the strength of the dollar." (p.117)

Credits from the creditor country to the debtor country "can be obtained if the program for restoring balance in the deficit country is considered reasonably promising." (p.119)

Finally, Roosa cites President Kennedy himself, who said in his speech of July 18, 1962: "We do not pretend that talk of long-range reform of the (international monetary) system is any substitute for the actions that we ourselves must take now." (p.122)

The same point of view is expressed with equal force in a very remarkable article published in April 1963 in the monthly review of the Federal Reserve Bank of New York, under the joint signatures of C. A. Coombs, Ikle, Ranalli, and Tungeler:

> Quite clearly, the United States Government has given the only possible answer to one horn of the liquidity dilemma, by asserting its firm determination to close the United States balance-of-payments deficit. Failure to do so would have disastrous consequences extending far into the future. While some progress towards reducing the deficit was made in 1961 and 1962, the time factor has now become a matter of major importance. (p. 115)

There is thus no possible room for doubt: The United States Government regards it as its own responsibility to restore the equilibrium of its balance of payments and does not think that this calls for a reform of the international monetary system.

Furthermore, an examination of the program for restoring equilibrium outlined by President Kennedy on July 18 confirms this statement at every point.

This program consisted of a series of measures: limitation of facilities for buying abroad, measures to encourage tourism in the United States, a projected tax on the purchase of foreign securities by United States residents, an effort at internal economic expansion designed to encourage investment in the United States by means of tax reductions, an effort to cut down military expenditure abroad and the cost of aid to third countries, and finally the obtaining of a standby credit of 500 million dollars from the International Monetary Fund.

All these measures were designed directly or indirectly to either cut down payment commitments abroad or increase income from abroad, in other words, by adjusting the balance of United States foreign commitments to the resources available to meet them, to do away with the balance-of-payments deficit.

The United States position is thus made quite clear. Having regard to its foreign exchange resources, the United States cannot, in present circumstances, meet the payments on all its foreign commitments. It must take government or administrative action, which President Kennedy's speech shows to be action to discourage expenditure abroad and to encourage income, so as to adjust its foreign commitments to its capacity to pay.

This formulation clearly shows that the United States Government has adopted the well-known principle, so often laid down after the First World War at the time when the transfer of German reparations raised the problem of Germany's balance of accounts, namely that effective transfers must be adjusted to the transfer "possibilities" allowed by the condition of the balance of payments.

The economists, Keynes and I

It is a fact that balance-of-payments theory has changed considerably since the time when Torrens, Ricardo, and John Stuart-Mill were teaching the theory of "comparative costs" in very different forms. Its gradual evolving, by scholars like

Pareto, Marshall, Edgeworth and more recently, Angell, Viner, and Haberler, has extended the analysis from the field of production to that of consumption and has substituted for Ricardo's simple theory of the "labor cost" the more general theory of "comparative advantages." With Ohlin and Samuelson, the theory now takes in all the internal and external factors of supply and demand that affect each article. It is a theory of exchanges between several markets rather than a specific international trade theory.

But the present evolution of the balance-of-payments theory is more important still. It results from the introduction of the concepts of "aggregate demand and aggregate supply," expressed in monetary units, as determining factors in the equilibrium of international transactions.

It was in 1927 in "Théorie des phénomènes monétaires" ("Theory of Monetary Phenomena") that I first came to consider the global volume of demand—calling it "total demand"—as the prime mover of shifts in economic equilibrium.

In 1945, in *L'Ordre social* ("Social Order"), this analysis was generalized, and I termed "balance of accounts of a given market in a certain period" the difference between the volume, expressed in monetary units, of the entitlements filled with and emptied of nonmonetary wealth, in this market, during the period concerned.[1]

On the basis of this definition, it appears that any excess of aggregate demand over aggregate supply generates an inflationary "surplus" that, *caeteris paribus,* is manifested on the supply side either internally through a price increase or externally through a balance-of-payments deficit. Except for characterized "underemployment" cases, the two phenomena are indissolubly linked, either one, if occurring in isolation, automatically drawing the other after it.

This analysis has the tremendous advantage of presenting the theory of international trade as a mere particular case of the general trade theory and of showing the inanity of any

[1] *L'Ordre social,* 2nd ed., p. 282.

distinction between domestic trade and international trade.[1]

But however different modern analysis may be from the analysis of the early masters who created political economy, it abides by their main conclusion and maintains that in a market economy there is a spontaneous tendency toward equilibrium in international settlements.

If, however, the mechanism that generates equilibrium is to govern balances of payments effectively, its mere existence is not sufficient. It is also necessary that the various elements of international transactions should in fact (given the sociological conditions of the moment and taking account, in particular, of the degree of cartelization and unionization that characterize existing social structures) be flexible enough so that the monetary influences that tend to shape them can actually influence their nature and degree.

It was this elasticity that Lord Keynes always denied. He regarded the various items in the balance of payments, and especially commercial exchanges, as established facts determined by facilities and needs resulting more from the nature of things than from influences exerted by exchange-rate variations or price movements.

I had a public controversy with him at the time of the dispute over German reparations. It is of real importance for economic theory, since it subsequently gave rise to a genuinely crucial experience from which any science that desired to be objective would draw decisive conclusions.

In September 1928 I had published a little book called: *An Economic Error: the Organization of Transfers (Une erreur économique; l'organisation des transferts).*[2] During the Assembly of the League of Nations at Geneva, in the late summer of 1929, the Director of the Institute of Advanced International Studies invited John Maynard Keynes (he was not yet Lord Keynes) and myself to expound our views to the students in two successive lectures, and subsequently to debate them together in public.

Keynes published his views in the *Economic Journal* of

[1] *L'Ordre social,* 2nd ed., p. 359.
[2] Published by Doin (out of print); reproduced herein, Chapter IV.

March 1929; mine were published in the same journal on
September 1929, and also in French in the Revue d'Economie
Politique under the title: "Mr. Keynes' Views on the Transfer Problem" ("Les idées de M. Keynes sur le problème des
transferts").[1]

The dates are important, since at the time they were
published Keynes' views, like my own, were forecasts based
on different "theories." And, as will be seen below, it was
only two years later that the facts made it possible to choose
between them.

In his article, Keynes expounded, with usual clarity, his
theory of the inelastic character of balance of payments:

> My own view is that at a given time the economic struc-
> ture of a country, in relation to the economic structure of its
> neighbours, permits of a certain 'natural' level of exports, and
> that arbitrarily to effect a material alteration of this level by
> deliberate devices is extremely difficult.
>
> In the case of German Reparations, on the other hand, we
> are trying to fix the volume of foreign remittance and
> compel the balance of trade to adjust itself thereto. Those
> who see no difficulty in this . . . are applying the theory of
> liquids to what is, if not a solid, at least a sticky mass with
> strong internal resistances.
>
> Historically, he adds, the volume of foreign investment has
> tended, I think, to adjust itself—at least to a certain extent—
> to the balance of trade, rather than the other way round, the
> former being the sensitive and the latter the insensitive factor.

I took the opposite view, maintaining, in particular, that
in certain conditions of a monetary nature "the most powerful 'natural' resistances cannot prevent the restoration of the
equilibrium of the balance of payments, even when the
equilibrium has been disturbed by events of a purely financial nature." I further showed that "the notion of a 'natural'
level of exports is a complete fallacy and cannot legitimately
be invoked."

This clash of opinions dominated the problem of the

[1] No. 4 of 1929 (Librairie du Recueil Sirey); reproduced herein, Chapter
IV.

German reparations, as today it dominates the problem of the balance-of-payments deficit of the United States.

In practice, if Lord Keynes is right, foreign payment possibilities must be regarded as an established fact, arising out of the nature of things. It is then a matter for Governments, by measures similar to those announced by President Kennedy in his speech of September 18 and to those that the United States Government is at present trying to apply through its policy of "self-restraint" in external payments, to adjust the amount of foreign payments to the amount of transfer facilities arising out of any credit items in the balance of payments, and especially the amount of exports.

If, on the other hand, I am right, a balance of payments can only be in lasting deficit if the monetary factors that tend to correct it have been eliminated or made inoperative.

The problem would then be to find out whether the present United States balance-of-payments deficit is not due to a distortion of the monetary mechanisms rather than to the inelasticity of its various elements. In the affirmative, the remedy would lie in the reconstitution of an effective international payments mechanism rather than in the manipulation, by government or administrative action, of the external commitments of the United States.

The facts of equilibrium

To settle the question, it is enough to look at the facts to find out whether it is true that in general balances of payments are virtually in equilibrium and to determine in what circumstances they have ceased to be so.

To discover whether international commitments tend in fact toward equilibrium, one must observe the various items when one of them is the subject of sudden and violent variation. If the theory of spontaneous equilibrium is true, we should observe a concomitant and compensatory variation in one or more of the other items of the balance of payments; and especially in the trade balance.

In the ensuing paragraphs, we shall look into this question, leaving aside any theoretical considerations.

1. If balances of payments could be the subject of a lasting deficit, no gold-standard system could last, as its gold reserves would gradually be completely exhausted by the drain of gold.

But we find in the long gold-standard periods that mark the second half of the nineteenth century and the beginning of the twentieth that gold movements are never continuous and that their amount is always small in relation to the volume of international trade that they serve to settle.

Thus, the balance-of-gold movements in France in 1912 was 220 million francs, or about 2 per cent of imports, which that year amounted to 8,200 million francs.

To judge the implications of this finding and the ones that follow, it must not be forgotten that they apply to a period when every individual in France and in most foreign countries could trade and travel as he pleased, that decisions whose consequences determined the balance of payments were arrived at independently of each other, that every Frenchman who drank a glass of port introduced a debit item into that balance, and that every foreigner who drank a glass of claret introduced a credit item. The existence of a lasting equilibrium between these countless debit and credit items could quite obviously not be the effect of chance.

2. In every period there have been rich countries and poor countries.

The rich countries were those that had invested capital abroad from which they derived substantial annual receipts in the form of interest and capital repayments, to which were nearly always added receipts in foreign exchange from freight, insurance, and banking services. All these credit items constituted invisible earnings in the balance of payments.

If, taking into account these invisible earnings, the balance of payments of these countries was to be in equilibrium, it is quite evident that the only visible item—the trade balance—would have to be in deficit.

The poor countries, which had borrowed abroad and generally had no substantial foreign income from freight, insurance, or banking, were in the inverse position. Their balance of payments could only be in equilibrium if their trade balance was in surplus.

This necessary inference from the theory of the existence of a mechanism that tends to ensure the global equilibrium of international commitments is quite contrary to common sense, which regards a favorable trade balance as a sign of wealth and an unfavorable one as a sign of poverty. This judgment is so hallowed that it leads to any reduction in debits or increase in credits being described as an "improvement" in the balance of trade. It is so absolutely accepted that I know of no government which does not regard itself duty bound to "improve" its country's trade balance in the sense indicated.

But if one looks at the international trade statistics for 1930, for example, one finds that the trade balance of France, the United Kingdom, the Netherlands, Belgium, and Switzerland showed a large deficit, while that of Germany, Poland, Rumania, Hungary, and Bulgaria showed a very large surplus.

This situation, which is so paradoxical according to the wisdom of the nations, constitutes a genuinely crucial test, since it can only be explained by the existence of a mechanism that tends to ensure the balance-of-payments equilibrium and demonstrates its power and effectiveness even in the most unfavorable circumstances.

3. The foregoing observations apply to a static situation. To prove the existence of a mechanism that tends not only to ensure the equilibrium of balances of payments, but also to restore it when it has been impaired, it is still necessary to observe what happens in periods when certain items of international commitments are the subject of sudden large-scale variations.

Variations of this kind are to be found mainly in commitments arising out of political decisions or manifestations of mass psychology.

Thus, under the Treaty of Frankfort of 1870, France agreed to pay Germany a war indemnity of 5,000 million francs of the day, and that amount was transferred during the years 1872, 1873, 1874, and 1875.

But the trade statistics show that from 1870 to 1914, France's trade balance, for the reasons given above, was always in deficit except in the years 1872, 1873, 1874, and 1875—and in those years only.[1]

This prodigious fact cannot be fortuitous. In itself it constitutes decisive proof of the existence of an effective adjustment mechanism.

4. The financial repercussions of the 1914–18 war furnish a particularly clear-cut example of sharp variations in one of the items in France's balance of payments.

During the war it happened that, in order to pay for imports essential to the war effort, the French Government requisitioned the bulk of foreign securities held by French nationals.

If there is a mechanism that tends to ensure the equilibrium of the balance of payments, and if that mechanism is effective, the deficit on France's trade balance after the war should be reduced by about the same amount as the annual income eliminated from France's balance of payments as a result of the sale of foreign securities.

But during the war, a quarter of the national territory was devastated. In 1921, it was still largely unproductive, although import needs for reconstruction were enormous and pressing. It was therefore highly improbable from the common-sense aspect that the deficit on the trade balance could be less than it was before the war.

In 1921, however, the deficit on France's trade balance, calculated in 1914-francs, that is to say in gold francs, was 575 million, as against 1518 million in 1912 and 1540 million in 1913. In other words, it had been reduced by two-thirds below the prewar level.

No mind, open to persuasion by facts, can be faced with a

---

[1] With the exception of 1904, when it was in balance, and 1905 when there was a surplus of 250 million francs.

reduction of this kind without recognizing it as irrefutable proof of the existence of a mechanism that tends to ensure the equilibrium of international commitments and as a measure of its effectiveness.

5. During the ensuing period, crises in the export of capital and the transfer of German reparations brought about sudden and large-scale variations in international commitments.

Reparations payments, which after World War I were not reparations in kind, but essentially financial payments, afford a particularly significant lesson for the present time, and especially for the United States, since they involve transfers with no economic origin that are therefore similar, *mutatis mutandis*, to military expenditure abroad or the cost of financial aid.

In 1924–25, France experienced its first major capital export crisis. This introduced a substantial debit item into the balance of payments. Immediately, the trade balance that, in conformity with the requirements of equilibrium as set forth in paragraph 2 above, was in deficit in 1923 to the extent of 2,256 million francs showed a surplus of 1,540 million francs in 1924.

But in 1928, M. Poincaré, at that time President of the Council of Ministers and Minister of Finance, restored order, French capital ceased to be exported, and on the contrary, massive foreign capital was invested in France. At the same time, the amount of German reparations came to swell the credit side of the balance of payments.

What was the result of this increase in credits? The trade balance, which had been in surplus during the capital export crisis, again moved into deficit, from 2,000 million francs in 1928 to 8,000 million in 1929, 9,000 million in 1930, and 11,800 million in 1931.

In the summer of 1931, however, the Lausanne Conference did away with German reparations. The French trade deficit immediately began to fall, from 11,800 million in 1931 to 10,100 million in 1932.

6. The variations in the German trade balance over the same period are even more edifying.

Following the stabilization of the mark, substantial foreign credits were invested in Germany. Their amount was considerably more, at any rate at the beginning of the period, than that of reparations payments. As theory would lead us to expect, the German trade balance showed a deficit of 2,532 million marks in 1924, 3,000 million marks in 1925, and 3,427 million marks in 1927 (the only exception was 1926, when a slight surplus of 413 million was recorded).

In the following year, reparations payments increased while foreign investments fell. The deficit was reduced to 726 million in 1928.

In 1929, a year of world crisis and exceptionally high interest rates in the United States, the inflow of foreign capital into Germany came to an end. With it, there disappeared the deficit on the German trade balance, which showed a surplus of 36 million marks.

In the following year the campaign for the abolition of reparations began in Germany. A new crisis of the mark was thought to be imminent.

The combination of these two factors generated a violent capital export movement. As always, the appearance of this new debit item in the balance of payments increased the trade surplus, which was 1,642 million marks in 1930 and reached the fantastic, and hitherto unimaginable, figure of 2,782 million marks in 1931.

This last variation in the German trade balance is of considerable importance for economic theory, because it settles *ex post facto* my 1929 controversy with Lord Keynes.

As stated above, Lord Keynes contended that "the economic structure of a country, in relation to the economic structures of its neighbors, permits of a certain 'natural' level of exports, and that arbitrarily to effect a material alteration of this level by deliberate devices is extremely difficult."

In my reply, on the other hand, I claimed that the most powerful "natural" resistances could not prevent the restoration of the equilibrium of the balance of payments even when the equilibrium had been disturbed by events of a purely financial nature. I argued further that the notion of a "natural" level of exports was a complete fallacy and could not legitimately be invoked.

In the field of experimental sciences a proposition is deemed to be true when it allows events to be accurately forecast and false when it is belied by events.

This criterion in the present case decisively shows that, contrary to the views of the great English economist, Germany's trade balance displayed extreme elasticity at the time, that nothing in its structure resembled a "natural" level of exports, and that any variation in foreign payments attributable to financial factors caused an almost immediate variation, by an equivalent amount, in the trade balance.

It is obvious that in this case it was the trade balance that had gone through a process of adjustment to effective transfers and that it would have been preposterous to claim that actual transfers must be adjusted to alleged transfer possibilities, which could be neither defined nor measured because of the balance of payments.

7. Observation of the United States trade balance leads to similar conclusions. Since the end of World War II, the United States has had heavy expenditure abroad. Such expenditure was economic only in part. It represented to a large extent international aid or assistance, afforded by the United States Government with a generosity unprecedented in the history of the world, and military expenditures that were the result of the presence of large contingents of United States armed forces in many parts of the world.

In addition to these noneconomic expenditures were those associated with the very considerable investments made by American firms in every part of the world, in particular in Britain and in the countries of the European Economic Community.

Briefly, interventions by the United States Government in foreign countries brought about a deficit of 3,547, 3,785, and 3,657 million dollars in 1962, 1963, and 1964 respectively, while the surplus of private expenditures over corresponding receipts amounted to 3,434, 4,307, and 6,360 million dollars for the same years, representing a total for these two items alone of 6,981, 8,092, and 10,017 million dollars, respectively.

Although the above figures do not take account of appreciable supplements that are to be found in the detailed statistics relating to the United States balance of payments, they are sufficient to demonstrate the existence of a very substantial balance-of-payments deficit attributable to "invisible" international transactions, i.e., transactions that do not figure in customs returns.

Now, over the same period, the trade balance of the United States showed a surplus (an excess of exports over imports) that was abnormally high: 13,950 million dollars in 1962, 15,024 million in 1963, and 17,885 million in 1964.

But there is more: the variations in this balance, i.e., 1,074 million dollars from 1962 to 1963, 2,861 million from 1963 to 1964, are in the same sense and of roughly the same magnitude as those in the invisible items that were 1,111 million dollars from 1962 to 1963 and 1,925 million from 1963 to 1964.

The exceptionally high trade surplus of the United States cannot be regarded as fortuitous; neither can the sense of the variations. But the two can easily be accounted for if one acknowledges the existence of a monetary influence tending to ensure global equilibrium in the balance of payments.

Thus, the situation of the United States is a fresh demonstration of the theory that the trade balance is not the result of structural influences, but the consequence of powerful monetary influences that affect economic behaviors in the public and private sectors, thereby tending to bring about global balance-of-payments equilibrium, taking account of all decisions of a noneconomic nature, even those due to international generosity.

The above remarks enable one to predict the effect of the measures of "self-restraint" through which the United States Government at present claims that it will resolve its balance-of-payments difficulties.

In an address before the National Industrial Conference Board in New York on April 16, 1965, I ventured to prophesy as follows:

> Some people believe that the balance-of-payments deficit could be remedied by a reduction in foreign expenditures such as military expenditure abroad or foreign aid, or again by control of foreign payments as under the all too well-known exchange control system. This is a fallacious hope. All precedents show that such reductions diminish the exceptionally high trade surplus of the United States but will not affect its balance of payments.[1]

These predictions were made even before the new system entered into force. Events will show whether or not the premises on which they were based were correct.

The facts of disequilibrium

THE DOLLAR "SCARCITY"

If the foregoing conclusions were regarded as valid in all circumstances, no balance of payments could ever show a lasting deficit.

During the past few decades, however, we have witnessed in several countries a prolonged and almost chronic excess of foreign-currency payments over foreign-currency receipts, leading, in certain cases, to the total exhaustion of foreign-currency reserves.

The most typical case is that of the Western European countries, which experienced a dollar "scarcity" between the end of the Second World War and 1958.

This scarcity was so marked and so permanent that it was regarded by most economists as a "structural" characteristic of the trading partners. In their view, it was the consequence

[1] Of course, they have temporary effects which are concomitant with the resulting repatriation of capital, but what I have in mind here is the lasting result.

of the economic strength of the United States compared with the economic weakness of the other Western countries. For purely practical reasons, unrelated to any monetary influence, these countries found themselves obliged, because of their impoverishment and American superabundance, to buy in the United States.

According to these same economists, the only way to counter this unavoidable disequilibrium was for the sole-creditor country to redistribute its surplus resources through a generous policy of grants or aid which the Marshall Plan typified.

This "structural" interpretation supported the Keynesian theory that "at a given time the economic structure of a country, in relation to the economic structures of its neighbors, permits of a certain 'natural' level of exports, and that a material alteration of this level is extremely difficult."

There is no doubt that its popularity was greatly enhanced by the enthusiasm that obtained at that time for the new doctrine that it entailed, in particular by stimulating American generosity beyond all foreseeable limits. There is equally no doubt that, in giving a doctrinal basis to the donation policy, it justified the relaxation of financial disciplines that had been so deplorably typical of certain debtor countries after the war, while it countenanced the unavoidably ensuing international begging which thus appeared supported by doctrinal justifications.

With all these consequences, the theory of the structural deficit gave the theorists the comfort that they so badly needed of an apparently scientific doctrine that enabled them to swim downstream rather than upstream, while at the same time gathering from the banks in passing all the joys of acquiescence.[1]

And yet, at the end of 1958, the "structural scarcity" of the dollar melted away like snow in the sun. Within a few months, it was replaced in most Continental European coun-

1 Obviously I refer here to intellectual joys and not to physical, practical benefits which are rarely the lot of the economist.

tries and in Japan by a superabundance of dollars, which has lasted ever since and is still continuing.

Yet, there had been no sudden change in the respective "structures" of the United States and Europe at the end of 1958. Although these structures are constantly changing, their evolution is slow and gradual. It cannot, therefore, account for the sudden change from a deficit into a surplus. But there is one feature of most of the Western economies that did change suddenly at the end of 1958, namely, their monetary system as a result of the general return to convertibility and the wiping out of domestic inflation in practically every country.

Now, within the country which it affects, inflation generates an excess of aggregate purchasing power that is in every respect similar to that which would have obtained if the balance of payments had been in surplus.

If the inflationary "surplus" exceeds the balance-of-payments deficit, it not only eliminates the monetary influence that tended to restore equilibrium in international transactions, but also generates an inducement to increase the foreign deficit, as a result of increasing domestic outlets. This reverses the stabilizing mechanism and inevitably generates a foreign currency "scarcity." The inflationary surplus thus fully accounts for the dollar scarcity in Europe during the period under consideration.

The monetary explanation is borne out *a contrario* by the sudden disappearance of the dollar scarcity wherever elimination of inflation has re-established in the debtor country the contraction in the aggregate purchasing power resulting from the foreign payments surplus.

Thus, the coexistence of the "structural scarcity" of the dollar and of internal inflation in the countries affected by such inflation, their simultaneous disappearance, without any appreciable changes in the structures wherever inflation came to an end, invalidate the structural explanation. On the contrary, they constitute presumptions that, though still only qualitative, are very strong, in favor of the monetary explanation.

THE EFFECT OF THE GOLD-
EXCHANGE STANDARD

However, while the transfer mechanism brought about a surplus in the trade balance of the United States, in conformity with all existing precedents, the moment it was no longer reversed by domestic inflation in countries affected by the dollar scarcity, the surplus that it generated did not suffice to restore equilibrium in the United States balance of payments.

Notwithstanding a trade surplus of 4,442 million dollars in 1962, 4,553 million in 1963, and 6,681 million in 1964, the United States balance of payments still showed a deficit of 3,605 million dollars in 1962, 3,261 million in 1963, and 3,053 million in 1964.

What is curious indeed and seems an exception to the rule is not that the trade surplus should have been quite exceptional, but that it did not rise to the level that would have secured balance-of-payments equilibrium.

Everything, however, becomes clear if one considers the modalities of the settlement of the external deficit of the United States, as they emerge from that country's statistical returns.

Part of the deficit was wiped out by redemption of earlier United States loans before the due date. Another part was settled by the sale abroad of American assets or by gold sales. The amount of such settlements, whose normal repercussions are felt on the volume of aggregate demand, amounted to 2,535 million dollars in 1962, 1,797 million in 1963, and 838 million in 1964.

But all the incremental deficit, i.e., 670 million dollars in 1962, 1,564 million in 1963, and 2,215 million in 1964, was settled in conformity with the gold-exchange-standard practices,[1] i.e., by an increase in dollar balances abroad, in other

[1] The gold-exchange standard differs from the gold standard in that it permits a Bank of Issue to create money not only against gold and claims expressed in the national currency, as under the gold exchange, but also against claims expressed in currencies payable in gold, i.e., in fact against dollars.

words, by a transfer to creditor countries of dollars that the latter countries were maintaining in the assets of their Banks of Issue.

Now, dollars cannot be used in Paris, Bonn, or Tokyo.[1] Therefore, the Banks of Issue which held them placed them back immediately in New York.

Thus, the debtor country received back the amount of its settlement on the very same day that such settlement was made. To this extent, therefore, there was no contraction in its purchasing power. From the point of view of aggregate demand, everything was happening as if there had been no deficit whatsoever as regards the amount under consideration.

One cannot, therefore, be surprised that the foreseeable trade surplus of the United States has not been sufficient to wipe out the United States balance-of-payments deficit. Long before this deficit could have been reabsorbed, the mechanism that tended to eliminate it had been made inoperative by the cessation of those transfers of purchasing power that, in the absence of the gold-exchange standard, it would have generated.

Thus, the mistake that one would make if one said that the increase in dollar balances abroad is the result of the United States balance-of-payments deficit becomes obvious. In terms of the problem of the chicken and the egg, it is the increase in the balances that is the cause and the residual deficit that is the effect.

All existing precedents enable one to state that if the whole of the deficit had given rise to an effective settlement, in other words if that part of the settlement that had been effected had not been nullified by transfer back to the United States, in the form of loans, of dollars paid to creditors, the trade surplus would have increased in the amount necessary and sufficient to reabsorb the whole deficit.

Thus, the "fact of disequilibrium" inherent in the maintenance of the deficit at the same level as the increase in the dollar balances abroad bears out in precise quantitative terms

[1] Subject, of course, to the wide outlets that the Euro-dollar markets have been offering recently.

the existence, the efficiency, the sensitiveness, and the power of the mechanism that tends to ensure equilibrium in the balance of payments through the transfer of purchasing power.

An outline of a
balance-of-payments theory

The facts of equilibrium and disequilibrium referred to in the two preceding sections enable one to note the existence and effectiveness, over a prolonged period, of a continuing tendency toward equilibrium in the balance of payments. Those facts are so specific and so unlikely that they cannot be accounted for otherwise.

However, the behavior and speeches of governmental and administrative authorities show that they do not accept in any way the contention that an efficient stabilizing mechanism does exist. In point of fact, they do not deny it, they just are not aware of it, even those who quote as their authority the classical contentions as they were taught them.

But this is not the position of the practical experts alone. In 1949, when I submitted to the "Congrès des économistes de langue française" (Congress of French-speaking economists) a report on "the present situation of international payments," I noted that nearly all my colleagues, including many of those whom I hold in high esteem and respect, were firmly convinced that the structural deficit contention was the correct one, and to them the belief in efficient monetary regulation of the balance of international transactions could only be accounted for by some rather sinful attachment to obsolete conformity.

It would be unfair not to recognize that their stand was supported by sensible arguments that the prevailing doctrine —Ricardo's theory as modified and improved upon by those who followed him—did not permit one to dismiss.

My opponents were all agreed in denying that variations

in aggregate demand and supply could have an effective controlling influence. They held the view that administrative decisions and trade negotiations influence commercial exchanges from day to day. They stressed the quasi-discretionary behavior of Banks of Issue and the contingency of open-market policies. In the face of such a sum total of arbitrary interventions, they refused to acknowledge the existence of an aggregate demand that would be effectively influenced by the net result of the balance of payments.

Those of them who made their criticism a little more specific were of opinion that the balance of international exchanges was so small in relation to internal aggregate demand —in particular in the case of the United States—that they refused to interpret it as anything more than a purely marginal influence that, in any case, was incapable of bringing about substantial price movements likely to influence international trade.

But whether we like it or not, the facts are there. In particular, the constant deficit in the trade balances of those countries that have no commitments to fulfil in foreign currencies and the constant surplus in the trade balances of those countries that effect important financial payments abroad are so widespread that they must be accounted for.

I am quite prepared to agree that the rough explanation provided by Ricardo and his followers ignores the problems raised by the undoubted effectiveness, in relation to balances of payments, of credit policies, and the consequences, which have always been noted, of inflationary conditions.

The above findings, which justified the reservations expressed by some of my colleagues, led me to reconsider the balance-of-payments theory.

I did so first in 1953 in a study entitled "Influences Regulating the Amount of Currency and the Institutional Problem of Money." But several readers complained that they had had real difficulty in following me through the details of a very complex analysis.

In order to meet their difficulties, I then attempted a more simple presentation, in an article on "The Theory of the Discount Rate and the Balance of Payments."

These two studies are reproduced hereinafter.[1] However, since they meet at least to some extent the criticisms which prevent enlightened opinion from recognizing the existence of a mechanism that accounts for the unquestionable facts revealed by observation, and as I am particularly anxious not to disrupt the continuity of my analysis, I shall try to outline the principle here and now. It goes without saying that the reader who requires strict reasoning should refer at least to the second of these two articles.

The basis of any *regulation* phenomenon can only be found in the feedback mechanisms well-known to cybernetics experts. The effect of the external deficit reacting on its causes tends to correct them. It is the mechanism of such a reaction that the theory should clearly bring out.

Any balance-of-payments deficit, by reason of the settlement that it gives rise to, entails in the debtor country not one consequence as classical theory has it, but two, namely:

A supply unmatched by a demand, which is in the nature of an "income-effect."

The reabsorption of cash balances up to the amount of the settlement effected, and therefore insufficient actual cash balances in relation to total desired cash balances. This is the "currency-effect" which is symmetrical with the foregoing.

These two effects, the "income-effect" and the "currency-effect," are not in opposition as is claimed by certain critics who are anxious to side with economic modernists, but on the contrary they are indissolubly associated in a fundamental complementarity, like the obverse and the reverse sides of the same medal.

The first consequence, the income-effect, tends, *caeteris paribus* as regards the aggregate volume of supply, to generate a fall in prices; the second, the currency-effect, tends to encourage a rise in rates on the money market.

I have demonstrated in the studies referred to above that

1 See Chapter VII.

the two movements are indissolubly linked and that if the one were to occur without the other, it would tend to induce it. To give a concrete idea of the reality of this relation, it is enough to resort to the expository device often used by Keynes and imagine that the debtor, in order to settle his foreign debt, offers on the market an assortment of articles made up in accordance with the composition of aggregate supply on the market. This assortment would consist of real wealth, the offer of which would tend to drive down prices, and claims, the offer of which would push up rates.

The income effect, through the diminution of aggregate demand inside the deficit country, will cause a disappearance of domestic outlets for a part of domestic production equal in value to the amount of the deficit, thereby releasing it for export.

If that part of production thus released for export finds a buyer at ruling market prices, the deficit will be corrected.

If it does not, domestic prices will tend to decline as a result of the reduction in aggregate internal demand.

This fall in prices would tend, *caeteris paribus,* to stimulate exports and discourage imports, thereby improving the trade balance. Such an improvement would make it possible to settle the deficit without drawing on metallic reserves.

But the rising money-market rate would end by coinciding, depending on the modalities of the intervention of the Bank of Issue on the market concerned, either with the discount rate or with the rate at which the Bank of Issue, under its open-market policy, buys obligations on the market. From that moment the securities offered and not demanded would be bought up by the Bank of Issue or the banking system that would create currency in exchange.

The general price level will then cease to fall and the trade balance will therefore cease to improve; the resources necessary for settlement, instead of being supplied by the market, will be drawn from the reserves of the Bank of Issue.

I stress that this analysis is very skimpy and grossly oversimplified. It is, however, sufficient to show that it is not true, as held by classical theory, that a balance-of-payments deficit necessarily generates an improvement in the trade balance.

In fact, the foreign currency needed to settle it may come from two distinct sources, namely the supply of gold or foreign currency resulting from an improvement in the trade balance, or a drawing on the gold and foreign exchange reserves in the assets of the Bank of Issue.

Access to each of these sources is marked by a "threshold" that in the first case results from the elasticity of international trade in relation to disparities between internal prices and foreign prices in terms of national currency, and in the second case from the level of the discount rate or the open-market-intervention rate in relation to the money-market rate.

If the discount rate or the open-market-intervention rate is appreciably higher than the money-market rate, the deficit in the balance of payments will mean an improvement in the trade balance. This improvement will continue so long as the rising-money-market rate fails to overtake the discount rate or the open-market-intervention rate, and the trade balance cannot fail to be established at a level which will ensure the equilibrium of the balance of payments without drawing upon gold, whatever may be the noneconomic items that go to make up this balance (including financial aid and military expenditure abroad) and whatever may be their variations at any time.

It is the resultant of all these items that constitutes the driving force and brings about the trade adjustment that will restore equilibrium.

On the other hand, as soon as the rising-money-market rate catches up with the discount rate or the open-market-intervention rate, the trade adjustment will come to an end. Prices will cease to fall in relation to foreign prices and the unrequited gap in the balance of payments will be settled by drawing upon the gold and foreign-exchange reserves of the Bank of Issue (or the banking system).

Thus the state of a balance of payments and the method

of settling the commitments that it implies depend solely upon the level of the discount rate or the open-market-intervention rate in relation to the corresponding money-market rates.

By keeping the former constantly higher than the latter, a country can always ensure the equilibrium of its balance of payments, whatever it may be, i.e., it can ensure that it is settled by improving its trade balance without any lasting drawing on its gold and exchange reserves.

However, it may happen—and indeed it frequently does —during periods of considerable budget deficit that the interest rate which would balance, by an offer of savings, the volume of Treasury bonds offered on the market is so high that it is not possible in practice to envisage a discount rate that would be in excess of the market rate of equilibrium. The budget deficit then generates an unavoidable state of inflation.

To sum up, it is the level of the discount rate (or the open-market-intervention rate) in relation to the rate of equilibrium of the money market which determines the balance-of-payments result and, in particular, determined whether it will be covered by an adjustment of the trade exchanges or by a drawing on the gold and foreign-exchange reserves.

In forming a judgment on this outline theory, it should not be overlooked, in the first place, that it has been deliberately simplified here, in particular by omitting a third possibility of settlement—which is by drawing on the production of gold mines, where such drawing is available in the monetary area concerned.

But that is not the difficulty. If the opinion of economists and of a number of monetary authorities is hesitant toward the theory set out above, it is because they find it hard to admit that contingent and ill-determined individual decisions should generate phenomena as strict as the facts of equilibrium described above.

Perhaps I may be allowed to remind them that nature, especially in the social and biological fields, abounds in ill-defined elemental phenomena that, by the law of large numbers, give rise to rigorous and well-determined macroscopic phenomena. The existence of the insurance industry is the most decisive proof of this.

As for the "sublety" of the theory, it is imposed by the strictness and the sublety of the facts to be explained.

But the most frequent criticism arises from the comparison of the volume of internal purchasing power and the international trade balance. It is said that if the latter is usefully to influence the former, it must be of the same order of magnitude, which is, properly speaking, unthinkable, particularly as regards the United States, where international transactions are only of marginal importance.

This argument, which would require a minute analysis, is not valid. The total amount of effective cash balances is constantly adjusted to the total amount of desired cash balances by the extremely sensitive mechanism disclosed by variations in the money-market rate. In the absence of open-market-intervention operations, the monthly pulsation of the rates ensures with extreme delicacy the supply of the desired cash balances. If open-market operations that generate undesired cash balances, and are therefore undersirable, disrupt this mechanism, the surplus will be reabsorbed by a reduction in the money-market rate in relation to the discount rate (or the open-market-intervention rate).

This constant and exact process of equalization between the actual cash balances and the desired cash balances ensures a constant and strict equality between aggregate demand and aggregate supply in the market concerned, as a result of the above-mentioned basic complementarity.

On the other hand, if the balance of payments shows a deficit, the reabsorption of cash balances by the purchase of the gold and foreign exchange needed for settlement causes an insufficiency of aggregate demand in relation to the global value of supply, up to the amount of the deficit. The phenomenon continues until the cause that provoked it has disappeared. The cumulative character of the process of domestic purchasing power contraction explains its absolute effectiveness, notwithstanding the rigidity of the structures and the resistances that any tendency toward a modification of existing situations confronts.

Thus, one understands why the discharge of international settlements can, with complete effectiveness and a sensitiveness similar to that of the money markets, adjust the trade balance to the requirements of the balance-of-payments equilibrium.

It is true that very many items in the balance of payments, in particular financial aid and military expenditure abroad, are not affected by considerations of rates or prices. But even so, acting in conjunction with all the debit or credit items, they bring about a favorable or unfavorable global balance. It is this resultant that triggers off the phenomena of regulation that inevitably adjust, with all their repercussions, whether direct or indirect, the elastic bulk of trade exchanges to the requirements of global equilibrium.

Thus, the facts of equilibrium set out at the beginning of this survey that, by their strictness, surprised the economists, appear as a necessary consequence of the theory and indirectly confirm it.

But the same theory is also confirmed, *a contrario,* by the lasting disequilibria that were not explained by the classical theory and that legitimately aroused doubts and reservations in regard to it.

States of inflation generally originate in borrowing operations in excess of the amount of savings that, in view of the rate of interest applicable, is available to meet them.

The placing of the loan is nevertheless secured by making the securities that represent it—generally Treasury bonds— eligible for discount or by means of purchases, effected by the Bank of Issue, at whatever price that bank is pleased to determine, under an open-market policy.

In both cases the monetization of the bonds offered and not taken up generates both undesired cash balances and an excess of aggregate demand that puts the balance of payments in deficit.

Because of the excess of the supply of bonds over demand for them, the market rate "sticks" to the discount rate.[1] The balance-of-payments deficit is settled by drawing on the gold and foreign exchange reserves, which it tends to exhaust.

Thus, the excess of borrowing needs in countries creditors to the United States has inevitably created the phenomenon described as the "dollar scarcity." Contrary to the almost unanimous belief of the experts, this was not a "structural" phenomenon, because it was solely the result of the inflationary situation resulting from the discount eligibility of Treasury bonds, offered in a quantity that exceeded demand for them, having regard to the interest rate attached to them.

Political conclusions

The foregoing analysis leads, in the case of the United States balance of payments, as in that of other countries, to a practical conclusion of the highest importance. It shows, in effect, that once the noneconomic items in the balance of payments have been determined, that is to say, those that are not more or less automatically determined by differences in prices or rates, the trade balance, notwithstanding alleged structural rigidities, adjusts itself with great precision to the level that will ensure equilibrium in the balance of payments, with the exception of the part settled in gold, which depends solely on the level of the discount rate (or open-market-intervention rate) in relation to the money-market rate.

We can be quite sure, with all the certainty afforded by the number and precision of the "facts of equilibrium" mentioned above, that any diminution by government or administrative decision in the debit items in the United States balance of payments (essentially military expenditure abroad

[1] Only from the moment when the commercial portfolio has been reduced to the level below which it cannot go. But we cannot here go into a detailed analysis of the phenomenon. Such an analysis is provided in the first of the above-mentioned studies.

and financial aid) would reduce the trade surplus by the same amount without in any durable way cutting down the deficit.

We can be equally certain that the measures contemplated by the United States Government to discourage operations that generate international debts and to encourage those that might create claims abroad will not affect the balance-of-payments result so long as the amount by which non-American Banks of Issue increase their dollar holdings every year remains what it is.

The volume of the outflow of gold will depend only on the level of the discount rate (or the open-market-intervention rate) in relation to the money-market rates.

So long as conditions remain what they are in the two spheres indicated above, an improvement in the United States balance of payments could only come about through a return to an inflationary situation in the creditor countries, and this is highly improbable at the present time.

In particular, the "self-restraint" measures introduced in the United States in 1965 will have no effect on the balance of payments except for a short period of time, but will reduce the trade surplus by a corresponding amount, subject to the reservation mentioned in the preceding paragraph.

All this leads to the certainty that governmental or administrative action, in the absence of authoritative control of the whole of international trade exchanges, cannot restore the equilibrium of a balance of payments that is in deficit.

This restoration of equilibrium, in the light of all the items that are determined in advance in international operations, can only be looked for from an effective currency regulation.

Only a reform of the international monetary system and a modification in the intervention rates of the Federal Reserve System can restore equilibrium in the United States balance of payments. All existing precedents support the contention that such steps would promptly restore equilibrium.

General comments

The foregoing views are drawn from the theory of international trade outlined in the present article that is developed in two more technical studies presented in the second part of this book.

In its present state, the theory is already confirmed by many qualitative and quantitative checks that allow the positive recommendations I have drawn from it to be taken as well established.

I do not overlook the fact, however, that my theory is complicated, and that on many points it requires thorough discussion.

Furthermore, its conclusions should be subjected to meticulous econometric checks, especially with regard to the fundamental assertion about the solidarity of price and rate movements.

To accomplish all these tasks, difficult theoretical and practical research is essential. Its findings, by providing new ways of convincing, would open up hope for a monetary policy understood and approved by all the great Western countries. Such a policy would secure their economies against accidents and would assure them of rapid and durable expansion.

It is astonishing that in a period that makes such extensive use of scientific research, that spends thousands of millions on exploring the nucleus of the atom, studies should be deferred that, if they were responsibly carried out in the banking laboratories whose creation is imperative, might spare the world the serious disturbances the continuance of present disequilibrium cannot fail to entail.

I would urge economists to reconcile themselves to the need, in the field of international settlements, for a "subtle" theory, capable of accounting for the precise and complex phenomena revealed by observation.

My own theory, which is imperfect, cannot be improved

unless it is submitted to the process of joint discussion and elaboration—a *sine qua non* of scientific progress. In the hope that it can be subjected to such a test, and to that end, I have attempted an unprepossessing statement of its components.

On a more general plane, it must be pointed out that the freedom of international transactions is only conceivable if individual behavior is confined within the limits imposed by currency regulating arrangements that tend to ensure the overall equilibrium without which no situation can be lasting.

Thus, freedom is not a free gift. It demands effective monetary systems. If we do not succeed in rapidly eradicating from our own system the perversions that impair the equilibrium of balance of payments, we shall inevitably be led to impose direct international trade control measures, which would seriously jeopardize the prosperity of the Western world, the well-being of its peoples, and all the principles that make its civilization great and unique.

2

THE 1949 PROBLEM,

FOCUSING ON THE

DOLLAR SCARCITY[1]

The improbability of a balance of payments in equilibrium

The main feature of a balance of payments in equilibrium is its extreme improbability.

The latter can be measured if one merely notes that any individual, in any part of the world, who drinks a glass of claret introduces a credit item into the French balance of payments, and that any individual in France who smokes a cigarette made of Virginia tobacco introduces a debit item. It is, therefore, the countless acts of individuals all over the world that combine at any given moment to make up international commitments. Now, these individuals act quite independently of one another and are never concerned with the impact of their acts on the aggregate balance.

[1] Text of a report submitted in 1949 to the "Congrès des Economistes de langue française" under the title: "Une cause du désordre mondial: l'état actuel du système des paiements internationaux." ("One of the Reasons for the Present World Disorder: the Present State of the International Payments System.")

This report was published in *Revue d'Économic politique*, No. 2, 1949, and in pamphlet form by the "Librairie du Recueil Sirey."

In such conditions, the quasi-balancing of the credit and debit sides represents a very exceptional situation from among all possible situations. The probability that it should exist at a given instant in time when nothing contributes to its establishment is very faint, probably of the same order as the probability that monkeys let loose in a typewriter shop to bang at random on the keyboards will reproduce all the books in the British Museum.[1] That such a situation should obtain in the relations between a great many independent monetary fields is more improbable still.

And yet the maintenance over several scores of years of certain systems of monetary convertibility and the absence, over a protracted period, of any defaulting in payments due to shortage of foreign exchange tend to demonstrate that a state of quasi-equilibrium has long existed between the international debts and the international claims of a great many nations.

Such a state of affairs could not be due to chance. If it existed, the reason was that an effective mechanism was ensuring its very existence.

The lessons of experience[2]

The foregoing conclusion must inevitably sound particularly trivial to economists. Indeed, all professors teach all the students in the world the balance-of-payments theory.

Yet over the past thirty years, and more particularly since World War II, all governments and monetary authorities, all trade agreement negotiators, and since the end of the war, those who negotiated reparations in kind under the Marshall Plan, have held the view that it was incumbent upon them to

1 This simile has been borrowed from M. Emile Borel, who uses it in his magnificent book on "*Le Hasard*" (Alcan).

2 The arguments submitted in this section have already been used in Section IV of the preceding chapter. However, I have retained them in order not to disrupt the inherent consistency of the 1949 text and to enable the reader to appreciate objectively its forecasting value.

establish, to safeguard, or to restore the balance of international commitments. Very few indeed informed them that their concern was futile. Over this period, everything occurred as if most economists had attributed only limited effectiveness to the balance-of-payments mechanism, on the ground that the tendency it demonstrated could not possibly have a real influence on the course of events.

The first problem raised by a study of the balance-of-payments mechanism is not whether such mechanism did or did not exist in the past—all economists agree that it did exist—but to determine its degree of efficiency at different periods in the past, in the circumstances in which it operated.

In an attempt to make this determination, I have considered a number of examples that are submitted hereafter:

1. First, a classical example that is often lost sight of. To the extent that the mechanism that tends to ensure balance-of-payments equilibrium is efficient, any country having substantial invisible foreign receipts (income from foreign securities, foreign incomes from freight, insurance or banking services) must have a trade deficit, and any country that is a debtor to foreign countries on account of similar commitments is bound to have a trade surplus.

Now, in 1930, Germany, Poland, Rumania, Hungary, and Bulgaria had a trade surplus, whereas Britain, France, the Netherlands, Belgium, and Switzerland had a trade deficit. This simple fact by itself proves that in 1930, notwithstanding the already advanced degree of economic organization, the mechanism tending to ensure balance-of-payments equilibrium was fully effective.

The traditional terminology that called "unfavorable" those balances that were in deficit, and "favorable" those balances that showed a surplus reflected the fact that public opinion did not suspect the existence of the forces that caused each balance to fall within one or another group. The intention that all the Trade Ministers of the world always proclaimed of turning their national trade balance into a "favorable" balance—i.e., to change it from the type of balance that Britain, France, the Netherlands, Belgium, and

Switzerland had in 1930 into the type of balance that Germany, Poland, Rumania, Hungary, and Bulgaria enjoyed at the same time—proves that they were as ignorant as public opinion regarding the theory of international trade.

2. Between 1870 and 1914, France, which was a wealthy country and held a substantial portfolio of foreign securities, always had a trade deficit[1] except in the years 1872 (+ 255 million francs), 1873 (+ 246), 1874 (+ 279), and 1875 (+ 345). Now, during those years the payment of the war indemnity that had been imposed on France under the Frankfurt Treaty introduced an exceptional debit item into the French balance of payments. The mere occurrence of a trade surplus is naturally not sufficient ground for me to claim that such a surplus is attributable only to the transfer of a war indemnity. Its mere existence, however, shows that during those years the trade balance reacted in the sense that theory could lead one to expect.

3. In 1917, the French trade balance showed a deficit of 21,000 million francs; in 1918, again a deficit of 17,500 million francs. But this latter deficit was covered in the amount of 17,000 million francs by the annual credits which Britain and the United States were extending to France.

In March 1919, such credits were ended. The trade deficit started to decline forthwith. In 1921, it had been reduced to 3,000 million francs.

Some will say that such reduction was inevitable, considering that the ending of Allied credits was leading to a stoppage of Government purchases abroad and thereby, *caeteris paribus*, to a reduction of the deficit by a corresponding amount. Such a contention would be immediately invalidated, however, if one considered historical evidence: Between 1918 and 1921, imports rose by 3,000 million francs, while exports increased by 20,000 million francs. Circumstances were therefore considerably changed. But the trade balance moved the way theory could lead one to expect.

Furthermore, one can see that it is not through a syste-

1 However, the trade balance was in equilibrium in 1904 and showed a surplus of 250 million francs in 1905.

matic reduction of imports, but through a massive increase in exports that the exchange and price mechanism promptly restored balance-of-payments equilibrium after World War I.

4. In 1912, the French trade deficit amounted to 1,518 million francs; in 1913, it reached 1,540 million francs.

Now, the 2,000 million franc deficit of the year 1921 represented, in terms of 1912–13 purchasing power, 575 million francs.

Thus, as early as 1921—i.e., two years after the end of the war—at a time when one quarter of the national territory—and by far the most export-oriented region—had been devastated, when domestic needs were vastly increased as a result of buoyant reconstruction activity, the trade deficit fell to one-third of its prewar level. It is in the light of this adjustment that the results brought about by the new procedures immediately after the Second World War should be appreciated.

5. In 1922, the French trade deficit was 3,177 million francs; in 1923, 1,918 million francs. But in 1924 and 1925, France was in the throes of a serious capital export crisis which introduced a considerable debit element into its balance of payments. As theory could lead one to expect, the deficit was turned into a surplus: of 1,702 million francs in 1924 and 3,214 million francs in 1925.

By mid-1926, the crisis came to an end, and an important movement of capital repatriation started. The trend of the trade balance was reversed and showed a deficit of 893 million francs.

The year 1927, a prestabilization period, was a most unusual one. In theory, one would have expected a deficit; in the event, however, the trade balance showed a 2,509 million franc surplus. It may well be that a more detailed study would make it possible to account for this surplus by an increase in the desired cash balances following the restoration of monetary stability. In any case, as early as 1928, a stabilization year, the statistical trend again developed strictly in accordance with expectations: The trade balance showed a deficit of 2,000 million francs.

In 1929, the capital repatriation movement was maintained and accentuated. Furthermore, France received very substantial payments by way of German war reparations. The trade deficit increased to 8,000 million francs. In 1930, it reached 9,900 million, and in 1931, 11,700 million francs.

In 1931, German reparations payments ended. The Great Depression was spreading to France, and capital repatriation was tapering off. In 1932, the deficit fell to 10,200 million francs.

Thus, during all this period of quick successive variations, movements in the trade balances nearly always conformed to what theory could lead one to expect. If they do not fully bear out the theory itself, they nevertheless constitute a convincing *prima facie* case in support of its validity.

6. The variations in the German trade balance during the same period are more edifying still.

Following the stabilization of the German mark, important foreign funds were invested in Germany. Their amount appreciably exceeded reparations payments, at least in the early stages. As theory could lead one to expect, the German trade balance showed a deficit: 2,532 million marks in 1924, 3,000 million in 1925, 3,427 million in 1927 (the only exception being 1926, when a slight surplus of 413 million marks was recorded).

Toward the end of this period, reparations payments increased while foreign investments were declining. The deficit was thus reduced to 1,726 million marks in 1928.

In 1929, the year of the World Depression when interest rates were exceptionally high in the United States, the inflow of foreign capital into Germany ended. With it, the German trade deficit disappeared, and the German trade balance showed a surplus of 36 million marks.

The following year saw the beginning of the German campaign for the abolition of reparations. A new crisis for the mark was regarded as imminent.

The combination of these two factors generated a violent capital export movement. As always, the emergence of this new debit element in the balance of payments led to an increase in the trade surplus, which rose to 1,642 million marks in 1930 and to the unbelievable, and until then inconceivable, figure of 2,782 million marks in 1931.

Outline of a theory

The foregoing results, which could be supplemented by a great many similar findings, could hardly be accounted for if one did not concede that there is a mechanism tending to ensure balance-of-payments equilibrium in a continuing manner. Such results also show that the stabilizing mechanism, in the factual circumstances prevailing during the whole period considered, was sensitive and effective, notwithstanding the resistances mentioned by Lord Keynes.

However, it is not sufficient to show that there actually exists a sensitive and effective stabilizing mechanism; its nature must be defined.

I have already observed that most teachings in the field of political economy include a theory of international trade.

As regards the inconvertibility system, there is unanimous agreement: Where there is a deficit, a rise in the foreign-exchange rate pushes up the level of foreign prices expressed in the national currency without affecting domestic prices— at least, not in a direct manner—and in any case without affecting them in a like degree. Thus, by stimulating exports and discouraging imports, the exchange-rate movement tends to restore balance-of-payments equilibrium.

Under the convertible currency system, the phenomenon is more complex. Classical explanations, based on a purely quantitative theory, seem to me difficult to accept. In Chapter 23 of "*L'Ordre social*,"[1] devoted to international trade, I expounded a theory that I believe to be more correct. It is based on the relations existing between gold movements and total income, all conditions remaining equal. Any bal-

[1] Librairie Medicis, 1967, 3rd ed.

ance-of-payments deficit leads to a demand for gold from the Bank of Issue. But such demand is expressed outside the market. If those who express it do not modify their cash balances, they have secured the resources necessary to purchase gold by means of a supply offer in the market. The deficit therefore causes, in the amount of such deficit, a supply that is not matched by a corresponding demand. Thus, the deficit tends to generate a fall in the general level of domestic prices that has the same effect as a rise in the exchange rate on the difference between the domestic price and the general foreign-price level and tends, like such a rise, to restore balance-of-payments equilibrium.

I also showed in the same publication that general price movements were associated with inverse movements in short-term monetary rates that, as a result of their effects on the current value of claims, acted on capital movements in the same sense as simultaneous price movements and like the latter tended to restore balance-of-payments equilibrium.

The effectiveness and sensitiveness of stabilizing mechanisms

However varied their shades of detail, all balance-of-payments theories have one feature in common: they all evince the existence of a stabilizing mechanism that derives from the effects on the relative price level in the various countries concerned of exchange movements under an inconvertibility system and gold movements under a monetary convertibility system.

Under both systems, the regulating influence generated by any balance-of-payments disequilibrium increases so long as the generating disequilibrium has not disappeared.

Hence, that all theories lead one to believe that so long as exchange movements under a system of inconvertibility, and gold transfers and their automatic effects on the general price level and interest rates in a system of convertibility, have not been prohibited, the stabilizing mechanism is bound to be effective since the force that it releases grows until such time as its desired result has been achieved.

These theories also show that the stabilizing mechanism is bound to be extremely sensitive, notwithstanding the "strong internal resistances" that caused Lord Keynes to be skeptical about it. Indeed, that the difference between the domestic price and the foreign price of a certain item, expressed in national currency, varies by an amount not in excess of the sum total of freight, insurance, and customs duties between the two countries concerned, is sufficient for the international exchanges to which such item gives rise to be completely reversed. Small variations in relative prices must therefore be sufficient to bring about very substantial changes in the trade balances.

In view of the two foregoing observations, one can hardly be surprised at the examples of concurrence adduced in Section II above. The mechanism tending to ensure balance-of-payments equilibrium does exist; it is bound to be effective and is of necessity extremely sensitive. It must therefore ensure equilibrium in international commitments, without any serious disturbance, regardless of modifications occurring in their components.

The perversion of monetary systems

The foregoing conclusion is only valid, however, to the extent that the conditions that govern the functioning of monetary mechanisms are effectively met.

Such conditions have been profoundly affected over the past few years by factual or legal circumstances whose consequences must be made clear.

INFLATION

The most important of all monetary perversions is the one that is generated by a deficit financed by the creation of purchasing power.

Any State that cannot secure through taxes or loans the revenue necessary to finance its expenditure is in a deficit. In such a situation, the settlement of expenditure, unless suspended, can only be ensured through the creation of monetary units that will increase by a corresponding amount the purchasing power derived from the sale of wealth offered in the market.

The regulating effect of monetary convertibility derives from the consequences of the balance-of-payments situation on the aggregate volume of the domestic purchasing power and, through such volume, on the level of prices and interest rates. Thus, settlement of a debit balance abroad entails the reabsorption of purchasing power by an equal amount, and thereby a certain shortage in the purchasing power available that is no longer sufficient to purchase, at ruling prices, the production offered in the market. The shortage thus generated causes movements in price and rate levels that tend to restore balance-of-payments equilibrium.

It goes without saying, however, that any creation of purchasing power reduces by an equal amount the reabsorption effect derived from settlement of the foreign debit balance. If the increment of purchasing power is in excess of the balance-of-payments deficit, it will reverse the influence that the latter tended to exert and will thereby tend, *caeteris paribus,* to augment the balance-of-payments deficit.

It is therefore solely the resultant of all the influences affecting the volume of the purchasing power effectively felt in the market that is the effective factor influencing the balance of payments. Wherever inflation is substantial and rapid, the purchasing power that it generates will always in fact be the dominant factor.

Where a number of countries experience a state of inflation concurrently, it is the rate at which inflation progresses in each of them—i.e., the ratio between the domestic deficit and aggregate demand—that, *caeteris paribus,* determines the rate at which prices increase and through such increase determines the amount of their mutual commitments and the resulting balance. A country where inflation, i.e., the rate at which prices increase, is small finds itself in the situation of a country with low price levels as compared with those where the pace of inflation is faster, and of a country with high price levels as compared with those where inflation is non-existent and prices are therefore stable. Thus, through movements in the general price level, aggregate variations in purchasing power will tend to put the country concerned in a creditor position vis-à-vis the former and in a debtor position in relation to the latter.

If the foregoing analysis is correct, it must stand up successfully to a test against the facts.

The facts show without any doubt that the pace of inflation was notably slower in the United States than in other belligerent countries. If international trade is indeed oriented by the variations in relative prices resulting from variations in aggregate purchasing power, then all belligerent countries must be in a deficit position vis-à-vis the United States.

Such is precisely the situation that is reflected with extreme rigor in the world-wide "dollar scarcity."

However, the uneven pace of the inflationary process is felt not only as between the European States and the United States, but also as among the European States themselves.

Switzerland and Belgium, for instance, are the two countries where prices have been most stable since the liberation. And it is obvious, for instance, that Britain's balance of payments still shows a deficit vis-à-vis these two countries, whereas it shows a surplus vis-à-vis countries where the pace of inflation has been faster.

The same situation would be revealed if one examined all bilateral balances.

Thus, the world-wide dollar scarcity and the relative scarcity of the various European currencies in each country clearly show that, notwithstanding efforts to plan it, international trade—even so far as England is concerned—is oriented only to a small extent by deliberate action on the part of governments. It remains for the most part oriented—as has always been the case in the past—by the price scale ruling in the territories of the various partners, a scale which, *caeteris paribus,* is the result of the aggregate demand that at all times is expressed in the various markets.

In the light of this finding, one cannot possibly claim that the regulating mechanisms have become inoperative, since despite governmental efforts and notwithstanding the intensification of economic rigidity in some sectors, they have generated in the case of the dollar and of certain European currencies the scarcity that theory could lead one to expect.

The monetary disorder that characterizes the present world situation must therefore be added to the illustrations presented in Section II as an additional, and probably the most decisive, proof of the efficiency of the mechanism of monetary regulation in existing economic structures.

THE RELEASE OF THE COUNTERPART OF MARSHALL-PLAN BENEFITS

Observation of the facts of the inflationary process enables one to predict the consequences of other perversions recently introduced into monetary mechanisms.

The cash deficit is not the only influence that perverts the balance-of-payments regulating phenomena. It can even be said that if all such deficits were corrected, the aid received under the Marshall Plan—taking into account the terms on which it is granted—far from eliminating the international disequilibria that make it necessary, would have the effect of perpetuating in the recipient countries a balance-of-payments deficit equal to the benefits received so long as such aid was maintained.

Indeed, the regulating effects of convertibility are felt only through the reabsorption of the purchasing power resulting from the settlement of a foreign debit balance. Now, the sale to domestic purchasers of a benefit obtained under the Marshall Plan does indeed drain away purchasing power that would be reabsorbed in a normal process of purchases abroad. But the release by the Marshall Plan authorities of such purchasing power under specific conditions enables the recipient State to disburse it, thereby eliminating any monetary influence that would otherwise tend to restore balance-of-payments equilibrium. From the monetary angle, and as a result of this release, everything takes place as though the external deficit filled by Marshall Plan benefits did not exist. There is nothing in the regulating mechanisms that could generate resources that do not have to be spent. The counterpart release therefore tends to perpetuate the existing state of things, i.e., to maintain the deficit that was intended to be financed by the benefit whose counterpart has been released.

THE MANAGEMENT OF THE INTERNATIONAL MONETARY FUND

In the minds of its initiators, the International Monetary Fund—which, incidentally, does not provide dollars any longer during the Marshall Plan period—was to replace the metallic convertibility system that they deemed too automatic. It is important to show that the conditions under which it has been functioning are such that the Fund is really a deficit-sustaining instrument.

When a member country of the Fund has to settle a debit balance abroad, it requests the Fund to provide it with the necessary foreign exchange against payment in its national currency. Under the convertibility system, the domestic currency thus expended would be reabsorbed. Its disappearance would set in motion the regulating process tending to correct the deficit. But the International Monetary Fund, being provided with such resources, invests them—subject to a ten per cent liquidity margin—in Treasury bills payable on demand and carrying no interest, instead of sterilizing them. As such, those resources, far from being reabsorbed, are placed again at the disposal of the State from which they come and can be spent forthwith by that State. Thus, no regulating influence is set in motion. Even if the public Treasury was in strict balance, the financing of a balance-of-payments deficit by the International Monetary Fund would, in such circumstances, tend to make the corresponding deficit a permanent deficit.

Administered in this way, the International Monetary Fund has every appearance of a convertibility system, but has none of its regulating virtues. It resembles the watches that little children wear—with hands and a winder, but no works inside the case. The Bretton Woods institution makes it possible to play the monetary convertibility game, but not to reap the benefits thereof.

The two alternatives: efficient planning of international trade or the restoration of monetary mechanisms

From the monetary point of view, the present situation is characterized by the maintenance in many countries of major cash deficits. It is therefore the relative magnitude of such deficits, not the balance-of-payments situation, that has the dominant influence on the direction of trade channels. So long as this situation obtains, monetary mechanisms governed by purely endogenous circumstances will not tend to ensure international trade equilibrium.

The last two paragraphs of the preceding section show in addition that even the disappearance of internal deficits would not restore the regulating mechanisms of the balance of payments, since the release of the counterpart of Marshall Plan benefits and the operating practices of the International Monetary Fund tend to perpetuate existing deficits.

In the existing state of international monetary relations, *there is no* reason of a financial nature for balances of payments to be in equilibrium. Their resulting balance, bobbing up and down like a cork in the water, is subjected to influences that remain completely unaffected by the transactions that determine them.

So long as this is the case, the equilibrium of international commitments, unless subjected to a spontaneous regulating influence, can exist only if it is deliberately and systematically brought about.

Indeed, it seems evident that the authors of the IMF Articles of Agreement had in mind the need for strict planning of international trade.

Article XX, Section 4, provides that the par value of the currency of a member shall be determined by agreement between the Fund and the member concerned.

Such a procedure would have made it possible from the outset to avoid disequilibria that could not be remedied. But in reality, events took a very different course. Each member communicated to the Fund the rate that happened to be in existence at the time when the new institution was going to start operating, and after a short period of reflection, the Fund concurred in all existing rates.

In so doing, the Fund was foregoing one of the most powerful influences that it could have wielded to restore international equilibrium.

It must be conceded, however, that the decision of the Fund authorities was inevitable. The determination of an exchange rate brings into question all the elements of domestic equilibrium and, in particular, price levels, wage levels, the allocation of productive activities, the social structure, etc. The rate to be selected depends not only on what does exist, but also on what may exist, i.e., on what the government is able and willing to do, particularly in the field of revenue. Is it conceivable that a small Board sitting in Washington could in such matters take the place of the responsible governments? The attitude of the Fund was the only possible one, but it let drop the main instrument of international planning that its Articles of Agreement had furnished.

It is true, however, that the basic text provides another line of action for the Fund authorities. Indeed, Article VII, Section 3 (a) lays down that where a member's currency is becoming scarce "the Fund shall formally declare such currency scarce and shall apportion its existing and accruing supplies of the scarce currency with due regard to the relative needs of members, the general international economic situation and any other pertinent considerations. The Fund shall also issue a report concerning its action."

The above provisions are supplemented by Article XII, Section S, which reads as follows:

"The Fund may, by a two-thirds majority of the total voting power, decide to publish a report made to a member regarding its monetary or economic conditions and developments which directly tend to produce a serious disequilibrium in the international balance of payments of members."

Is it possible that all those who have to handle the realities of economic policy, all those who are aware in particular of the host of interests that are affected by the slightest decision in the field of international trade could see in such recommendations, even made publicly, a serious means of correcting international disequilibria? Recommendations made by the Fund would be regarded as wishes deserving consideration and esteem, but not as injunctions that could result in effective action.

There remains action that the governments themselves may be disposed to take. There again, if one is to be realistic, one must recognize that the means available at present are only of very limited effectiveness, at least in the present state of our political structures.

In order to stimulate exports, it is necessary in the first instance to produce those articles that are likely to be exported and therefore to allocate to their production an adequate proportion of the inputs available, even though the domestic market may offer more profitable outlets than export markets. Such a necessity requires that the State should allocate raw materials, capital, and above all labor, by way of authoritative decision. This may perhaps be done successfully and with a reasonable degree of efficiency under a totalitarian regime; but under the kind of regimes that we have, economic organization is so difficult that it never achieves more than partial completion of export targets.

Furthermore, in order to correct a deficit it is not sufficient to produce exportable wealth—foreign countries must also purchase it. Now, the only means of inducing foreign countries to buy one's products is to offer them at a price lower than the prices asked by competing suppliers. But any policy of export subsidization is expensive and the results that it can yield are therefore limited. Once they have been attained, the only thing left to restore balance-of-payments equilibrium will then be to reduce the level of authorized imports to the level of feasible exports. In claiming to restore international trade equilibrium, international trade planning will in fact always result in restricting international trade. It will, as always in the past, be nothing but a policy of economic autarky.

Thus, within the framework of the Western European political regimes, the planning of international trade can have only superficial and always Malthusian effects.

If this conclusion did not seem to have been sufficiently substantiated, the mere analysis of the British balance of payments would confirm it.

No country has attempted more seriously than Britain to plan its international trade; no country has devoted to this task so much ability and civic spirit.

Yet, although Britain has considerably improved its overall balance of payments, it has not succeeded until now in achieving the kind of geographical distribution of its exports that would provide it with the foreign currencies that it needs.

The former result, i.e., the improvement of the overall balance, has been secured by restricting with unprecedented courage the aggregate purchasing power. This result therefore confirms the effect of the volume of purchasing power on the international trade balance and thereby shows the efficiency of the regulating phenomenon whence the convertibility system derives all its virtues.

The latter result, i.e., the imperfect distribution of partial balances, is the inevitable consequence of the uneven rates at which inflation progresses in the various partner countries in accordance with the mechanism analyzed above. This result is therefore attributable not to any deliberate orientation of trade channels, but to their automatic orientation due to the influence of price differentials.

It cannot therefore be contended that under present conditions a substantial part of Britain's foreign trade is effectively controlled.

When God has something difficult to be done, he entrusts it to the British, but can the other nontotalitarian countries expect to succeed where Britain has failed?

In the present situation of Western Europe, balances of payments are no longer determined by the automatic regulation of monetary convertibility nor—at least, not to any material extent—by the deliberate action of governments.

They are therefore given up to chance and doomed to disorder.

If order is to be restored in the world, there are only two possible solutions: monetary convertibility or totalitarian disciplines, without which no planning can achieve results.

Conclusion: some reflections on political psychology and a suggestion in the field of political economy

Most of the acts accomplished in the field of political economy since the war are based on the implicit contention that balance-of-payments regulating machanisms have become inoperative and will remain so for a prolonged period.

The Yalta agreements, for instance, provide that reparations are to be exclusively in kind. To those who are aware of the inconvenience of such payments, which cannot be adjusted to the most urgent needs of the recipient countries and exclude any triangular procedure, the decision can only be accounted for by the profound belief of the statesmen who made it that any system of financial transfers was doomed to failure.

The Potsdam agreements bear out this conclusion. Indeed, they lay down (Article III, Section 19) that as regards Germany "the proceeds of exports from current production and stocks shall be available in the first place for payment of imports approved by the Control Council." The above text has been interpreted as ruling out the feasibility of reparations payments out of current production, it being impossible to expect that German exports could ever yield resources over and above those required for payment of essential imports.

The famous address in which General Marshall announced the generous offer of the United States Government, at Harvard on June 5, 1947, includes the following sentence: "The truth of the matter is that Europe's requirements for the next three or four years of foreign food and other essential products—principally from America—are so much greater than her *present ability to pay* that she must have substantial additional help or face economic, social and political deterioration of a very grave character."

All the above texts show that the authors accepted as a fact the prolonged inadaptability of the balances of payments to the new debit elements that could be expected. They did not envisage any other solution than the adjustment of their policies to existing payments capabilities and had no hopes that such payments capabilities could be adjusted to the requirements of their policies.

Assuredly, at the time of the Yalta and Potsdam agreements, at the time when General Marshall's offer was formulated, balances of payments were considerably inelastic. But, as has been shown in the case of Britain, in countries other than Russia their inelasticity did not result from any structural change in economic reality. It was the outcome of a system that had disrupted the functioning of the regulating mechanisms, for reasons that one must concede were legitimate, since the purpose was to avoid the social consequences of inevitable deficits. It does seem that in the postwar period most statesmen were in agreement with the consensus of public opinion and considered as permanent a situation that in fact was only fortuitous and could, in any case, as the examples of Italy and Belgium showed, be promptly corrected.

It would be interesting to try to determine what influences led public opinion to accept as a dogma the indifference of economic reality to the functioning of regulating mechanisms. It is probable that factual circumstances played an essential part. Impressed by what he can see, the layman, however enlightened, denies what he cannot watch, above all when its existence has never been known to him.

An essential feature of the Bretton Woods Articles of Agreement is that none of the chapters of this instrument either deals with the regulating virtues of the mechanism that it was intended to set up or attempts to govern the relations between the Fund and the central Banks of Issue.

Similarly, future generations will be astounded when they read Volume I of the *Interim Report on the European Recovery Programme* (Organization for European Economic Cooperation, Paris, December 30, 1948). This document, which deals with the method likely to restore, before 1952, the balance-of-payments equilibrium of all the Marshall Plan recipient countries, envisages a multiplicity of efforts toward systematic harmonization and adjustment, but does not seriously contemplate resort to the mechanism of monetary convertibility. Everything was conceived as if in the minds of the authors of the report such mechanism did not exist.

However, the alternative is a simple one. No one—not even the authors of the Interim Report—believes that the planning measures envisaged in the report will make it possible to restore equilibrium in the balances of payments concerned before the Marshall Plan comes to an end.

Yet the facts that I have adduced show in all certainty that the mechanism of convertibility, which has always been effective in the past to ensure the restoration of international equilibria, would still be so at present.

If therefore it is really desired that an end should be put to the present disorder in Europe, there is only one possible solution: the restoration of monetary convertibility at the earliest possible date in the greatest possible number of countries.

The method to be followed to that end is no new one. It was tried and tested many times by the Financial Committee of the League of Nations between 1920 and 1930, under the auspices of the Bank of England. It yielded decisive results. It involves three main lines of action: Cash resources should be balanced, the economic situation should be put on a sound basis, the reserves of the Bank of Issue should be reconstituted, while the par value at which convertibility will be restored should be determined.

The present situation, however, comprises an entirely new feature.

In the past, attempts to restore a sound situation were bound to be a slow process because in each case the resources necessary for restoration of the cash balances could only be secured through the floating of a loan in the major international markets. The generosity of the United States creates for a limited period of time a situation unprecedented in the history of the world, since it would make it possible, under the Marshall Plan, to restore simultaneously and almost immediately all the reserves of the Banks of Issue concerned. To that end, the only requirement would be that instead of being used to secure a number of varied benefits which are likely, of course, to lead to a most welcome improvement in the material situation of the recipient countries, but not to restore lasting equilibrium, part of the resources of the Plan should be earmarked for the purchase of gold to be delivered to the Banks of Issue of the recipient countries.

To be sure, the restoration of metallic reserves would not in itself be sufficient to restore monetary convertibility in a permanent way. But within the framework of a general program for the restoration of sound conditions, which it would both crown and sanction, it would open the way for the early re-establishment of a system likely to lead to what planning endeavors will not bring about: continuing equilibrium in all balances of payments.

If it is therefore desired that the Marshall Plan should effectively restore order in Europe, it is necessary in the first instance to convince the European States that convertibility alone can promptly and efficiently solve the problem confronting them.

If this can be achieved, the United States must be persuaded to agree to allocate to gold purchases a substantial part of the credits they grant within the framework of aid to Europe.

Lastly, the European States must be persuaded that if they are to receive any part of Marshall aid in the form of metal, they must apply, each within its own territory, the traditional procedures for the restoration of sound finances.

Then, and then alone, can one be assured that the Marshall Plan will attain its objective and that order will be restored in Europe before the Plan comes to an end.

3

INTERNATIONAL TRADE

IN 1948: APPEARANCE

AND REALITY

The report of the Central Wool Committee for 1947 has been a real revelation.

It has taught me the details of a system which I knew only by name: the Import-Export plan that was proposed to you in 1947 by the public authorities.

That such a system could have been proposed to you is the essential element of the problem I am to deal with here. It should enlighten all those who reflect on the present situation.

Before the war, as Director of the French Treasury, I had to negotiate quite a few international financial agreements. In those days, we were still governed by the national bilateral system, which means that one was only concerned about balancing trade between pairs of contracting countries, for instance France and Germany, or France and Belgium. Even at that time, I felt how arbitrary and illogical was a system that, disregarding global equilibrium, was concerned only about a set of bilateral equilibria. But much progress has been made since. We are no longer governed by a system of bilateral national equilibrium. If I have rightly understood

Lecture presented to the XXVIth General Assembly of the Central Wool Committee in May 1948.

the scope of the Import-Export system, we have now arrived at a system of bilateral equilibrium in each trading sector, which means that the main concern is to ensure equilibrium within each trading sector as regards the exchanges between pairs of countries. This is a stage further which is of great importance. The next one, if we continue in the same direction, will be the system of individual bilateral equilibrium, which means that a doctor will be able to buy footwear only on condition that he tends the shoemaker and on condition that the shoemaker obligingly contracts the particular ailment that the physician treats! We have not quite reached that stage yet, but the important fact is that we have reached the system of occupational bilateral equilibrium.

Why has this system been proposed, allowing you to import to the extent that you export, thereby obliging you to look to your own exports in order to find the foreign currency you need for purchasing the raw materials for the manufacture not only of products intended for export, but also of products required for domestic consumption?

The reason is extremely simple: It is because those in the Ministry of Finance, notwithstanding all their zeal, are in the same position as the most beautiful girl in the world, who cannot give more than what she has. There is nothing like having to manage a foreign currency reserve to develop a sense of realism. It makes you "discover" a whole set of basic principles that in general economists are unable to comprehend, such as in particular that you cannot have your cake and eat it, that once it is gone, it is gone. The basic principle as far as currency matters are concerned is that under the systems that we have instituted, when you have exhausted your reserves, well that is the end of them. If you then want to go on buying abroad, you must find the foreign currency required for payment. What has been suggested to you is a means to acquire such foreign currency, and in a moment we shall see what the consequences are. But the salient feature of the present time is that we have created a civilization, or allowed a civilization to be created, in which, in order to be able to provide the French with the textile products they need, you must previously have persuaded a sufficient number of foreigners to buy your products in such quantity that the aggregate value of your exports will cover all your requirements of foreign raw materials, including those intended for domestic consumption.

One could argue that basically this situation is a consequence of war and of the disturbances engendered by war, that it would not exist if we had continued living in the state of quasi-equilibrium that we had achieved prior to 1939.

What was the situation before the war—rather, just before the war (because then we were already moving toward the present situation), but during the 1930's and, above all, prior to 1914—when such a system did not exist? At that time, it was inconceivable, and no one had ever imagined, that a foreign exchange shortage could be invoked to stop someone who wanted to purchase abroad. The possibility of effecting payments abroad at any time in any foreign currency was one of those daily marvels on which we felt entitled to rely. This was a basic truth to us, like the existence of air or light, an ever-renewed miracle that had ceased to amaze us. When one made purchases abroad, all one had to do was to instruct a bank to make payment, and the foreign exchange required for settlement was always available.

Was this a natural state of things, attributable to the economic order existing at the time? In order to appreciate the situation, one needs to reflect upon the conditions that must be met if one is always to be in a position to settle one's debts abroad. At any time, the foreign exchange inflow must roughly equate the amount of foreign payments to be effected. Now, what do assets and liabilities consist of in such a case? To get an idea, just think that any individual who, somewhere in the world, drinks a glass of claret introduces a credit item into the French balance of payments, and that any person who somewhere in France smokes a cigarette made of Virginia tobacco or wears a jacket made of English cloth, introduces a debit item. In other words, the balance of payments is the resultant of countless activities by individuals who act in a completely unrelated manner and never worry about the effects that their individual acts may have on the overall equilibrium. Now, every year the sum total of unrelated acts used to result in an equilibrium such that, before 1914, gold movements—by which one can measure the difference between the debts to be settled and the amount of foreign exchange available for settling them—exceeded 250 million French francs per year only very rarely, as against a total volume of more than 6,000 million francs on both the credit and debt sides of the ledger.

What did this mean, if not that the balance of payments was roughly in equilibrium? Everyone acted free of any control whatsoever, regardless of what others did. How then could it be that this sum total or simultaneous unrelated actions should always have resulted in such overall equilibrium?

My conclusion is that such equilibrium, which *did* come about, could not have been fortuitous.

It is not my intention here to give you a lecture on political economy, that would be extremely boring. But your President has told me that the time available to us is a little longer than I had thought. So I should like, with your kind permission, briefly to recall the nature of the mechanism that, as all economists agree, tended to secure balance-of-payments equilibrium.

What did this mechanism consist of?

Under the system of convertibility, the exchange rate was a fixed one and fluctuated only between the gold import and export points. When a country had a deficit vis-à-vis other countries, its foreign exchange debts were in excess of its foreign exchange claims. In order to effect payment abroad, one asked the Bank of Issue for gold. By so doing, one reduced purchasing power in the debtor country. This purchasing power was transferred in the form of gold to the creditor country, where the aggregate purchasing power increased as a result. This twofold movement caused a slight depression in prices in the debtor country and a slight increase in prices in the creditor country; the difference in relative costs that was felt throughout the economy tended to restore balance-of-payments equilibrium.

Under a system of inconvertible currencies (and before the war, deficits had caused widespread suspension of convertibility), the phenomenon was slightly different. Purchasing power could neither be exported nor imported. Each country was, so to speak, a trap for purchasing power. When one had to effect payments abroad, one requested foreign exchange, and this tended to increase the exchange rate of the currency of the creditor countries. Variations in exchange rates engendered variations in relative costs analogous to those generated by gold transfers under the metal convertibility system, and these variations in relative costs tended to restore balance-of-payments equilibrium.

I know full well that some of you, and even a large part of public opinion, smiled benevolently when this mechanism was referred to and said: "All this is theoretical talk. Reality does not worry about such variations in relative costs. One would need a microscope to detect them. They do not affect the major trade flows, for the latter do not respond to such negligible influences."

Let us look a little more closely at prewar realities and try to determine the degree of efficiency of this mechanism, which through variations in relative costs tended at each and every moment to secure equilibrium in international commitments. You are all aware that very small differences in relative prices are enough to reverse trade flows and that the moment the foreign price of an article, expressed in francs, is less than the domestic price, one buys everything abroad and stops buying in the domestic market—provided, of course, that there are no quotas. Inversely, the moment the price of the domestic product is lower than that of the foreign product, expressed in domestic currency, foreign orders pour in whilst in fact it is extremely difficult to manage to export a product of the same quality as the foreign product when such product sells at a higher price in the domestic market than abroad.

After all, the whole philosophy of this stabilizing mechanism is quite simple. Where quality is comparable, price differences are the factor determining trade flows.

This is in fact what most of my fellow economists teach their students. The only surprising thing is that they have no great belief in it, that most of them give the impression that those are truths appropriate to teaching but are no good for being applied in the serious business of everyday management.

Let us look at the facts.

I have studied the French trade statistics from 1870 to 1914.[1] First, one notes that, except in five years, it always shows a deficit. Why? Because throughout this period, France was a wealthy country with an important portfolio of foreign securities, that had receipts in foreign currencies accruing to it in the form of interest and dividends, insurance premiums, banking commissions—a country, therefore, that had substantial invisible foreign earnings. If the balance of payments was to be in equilibrium, the trade balance had to show a deficit, since every year there was an important foreign currency inflow which did not appear in the trade balance. All the wealthy countries—Britain, France, the Netherlands, Belgium, Switzerland—had trade balances that showed a deficit, and all the poor countries—Poland, Bulgaria, Hungary, and Rumania—had trade balances that showed a surplus, a fact which by itself already proved the existence and efficiency of a mechanism that tended to ensure balance-of-payments equilibrium.

The trade deficit was therefore a manifestation of wealth, contrary to what is commonly believed. And to turn the trade balance into a favorable trade balance was, in fact, to convert a rich country into a poor one. In order that a trade balance should show a surplus, it sufficed to contract debts abroad. In 1919, at a committee meeting concerned with "improving" the rade balance of France after World War I, my former mentor, M. Colson, observed as follows: "There is a very sure means of quickly turning the French trade balance into a favorable trade balance, and that is to state that

[1] *Bis repetita placent.*

every year France shall pay Germany a reparations indemnity equal to that which we are entitled to demand."

I was telling you that I have examined the French trade balance between 1870 and 1914. It always showed a deficit except in four years: 1872, 1873, 1874, and 1875. Now, these four surplus years were those in which France paid Germany the war indemnity that Germany had demanded after our defeat in 1870.

This is a peremptory illustration of the existence of this mechanism that tended to determine balances of payments globally by ensuring their equilibrium: We make payments abroad; our trade balance forthwith adjusts itself and produces the necessary foreign exchange surpluses, and the moment the payment comes to an end, the balance again shows a deficit, as previously.

There is another example that is no less typical and more closely resembles present reality: In 1917 and 1918, the French trade balance showed a deficit of 20,000 million French francs, which approximated so many gold francs. During those two years, our British and American allies supplied us with 17,000 million francs of credits, so that the deficit amounted roughly to the prewar deficit, plus the above-mentioned credits that had been extended to us to effect purchases abroad.

One fine day in March 1919, our British and American allies decided to cease granting us the credits. Whereupon our trade balance, which lost this credit item, began to change and in 1921, at a date closer to the end of the war than the present date is to the end of the Second World War, the French trade deficit had been reduced to 2,295 million francs: the variation had been almost exactly in the amount of the credits lost to our balance of payments.

In other words, within a period of two years, the French trade balance had adjusted itself very closely, as you can see, to the new situation resulting from the elimination of foreign credits.

But more remarkable still, the 2,295 million francs deficit recorded in 1921 was the equivalent of roughly 575 million prewar francs, having regard to the intermediate rise in prices. In other words, in 1921, at a time when one-fourth of the national territory had not yet been restored to production (because, although devastation in the last war was much more widespread than destruction in the First World War, one must not forget that the destruction wrought during the First was particularly serious and affected the best exporting regions of the national territory—you should know better than anyone), in 1921, then, that is two years after the end of the war, the French trade deficit had declined to one-third of its 1913 level, in terms of purchasing power.

In fact, in 1913 the deficit had amounted to 1,540 millions of 1910 francs, and in 1921 it was 575 millions of 1910 francs.

Does this not afford decisive evidence of the efficiency of this exchange and price mechanism? Indeed, such a mechanism cannot but be efficient since the exchange and price variations continue until such time as the result which they tend to bring about materializes. It is therefore not possible that it should fail to restore equilibrium.

I hope that these examples—and I could adduce many more because the efficiency of this mechanism does not suffer any exception—will persuade you that the mechanism of combined exchange and price variations as it operated before the 1914 war and in the interwar period, in fact ensured overall equilibrium of balances of payments in a permanent way. It gave you the assurance that when you had a payment to effect abroad, you could come by the necessary amount of foreign exchange and no one needed to be concerned about its being generated.

Compared with this finding, what is the present situation? It is precisely to enable you to assess it that I made a point of adducing these few historical considerations before you.

The present situation is the result of a number of successive measures, the first being widespread resort to exchange controls.

What are exchange controls? Exchange controls are a system which prohibits, under penalty for nonconcurrence, any contractual arrangements expressed in foreign currencies at a rate different from the official rate.

There would be much to be said—and I believe it would be of considerable importance—on the appearance of exchange controls in the world. They were first introduced in Germany. Paradoxically, the Western powers—the United States, Britain, and France—largely contributed in 1931 to their establishment through the standstill agreements, thus making the advent of Hitler possible—but that is another story.

Exchange controls eliminated convertibility and pegged exchange rates. As a result of this twofold effect, they did away with the mechanism that tended to ensure balance-of-payments equilibrium. The consequence was that balances of payments were no longer in equilibrium.

The first consequence of the pegging of the German exchange rate, for instance, was that the Franco-German trade balance was no longer in equilibrium and that Germany ceased to pay for its purchases in France. We had to protect ourselves, of course, and to do so we invented the clearing system. In 1934, I personally negotiated with Dr. Schacht the first clearing agreements to which France was a party. The Franco-German clearing system was a defensive reaction. Germany was no longer paying our exporters. We told the French who had settlements to effect in Germany: "Instead of paying the Germans, you shall pay the French whom Germany has not paid."

But the clearing system not only disrupts the stabilizing mechanism, it also tends to reverse it, thereby tending to aggravate the deficit which first made it necessary. Germany had an increasing interest in making its purchases in France, but fewer and fewer possibilities of making settlement.

The system was preposterous. I feel I am entitled to say so since I contributed to its establishment, because one could not do otherwise than resort to it. This was only a defensive reaction, and anyone with a sense of reality knew that there was no other way out. Politics is the art of choosing the least among several possible evils. But the least evil solution was a hateful one, which is a serious flaw, and what is worse, it was preposterous because it tended to aggravate the evil.

Since then, we have done much better!

Indeed, we have made this situation a general one. Clearing agreements were bilateral instruments. We turned them into a great multilateral instrument: the International Monetary Fund. The Fund is an instrument strictly analagous to the Franco-German clearing system. It has perhaps fewer defects because it is a multilateral device, but you know full well that one does not arrive at a surplus by adding deficits together.

The International Monetary Fund carries all the consequences of a bilateral national clearing system: It destroys the stabilizing mechanisms and thereby does away with any influence tending to secure balance-of-payments equilibrium.

What is basically the essence of the system? It resides in the fact that it eliminated any adjustment mechanism through variations in relative prices.

Let us take a concrete example. You have all known the situation which existed prior to the latest devaluation. You know full well that, in view of the French and United States price levels, it was impossible to export from France any products likely to be available in the United States. Maintenance of that rate of exchange was the most efficient measure which could have been imagined to sustain the French balance-of-payments deficit and thereby to generate the dollar scarcity which is the root of so many of our evils.

It is a curious fact that one should create the evil one complains about so bitterly and that one should cling desperately to the system that sustains it.

When one discusses with economists, one finds that they often agree on the foregoing conclusions. And they say: "We admit that we have disrupted the stabilizing mechanism. But you are behind the times. This stabilizing mechanism belongs to the days when exchanges were strictly on an individual basis, when international trade flows were not 'organized'. We concede that exchange controls and the International Monetary Fund have disrupted the stabilizing mechanism; but on the other hand, we have established a system under which we can substitute deliberate order for the spontaneous order generated by free exchange and price movements, and this deliberate order is imposed upon the world by planning."

What I now would like to investigate with you is the exact degree of planning which exists in the world in which we live, and whether in fact the work of planning that is adduced by way of justification and apology for exchange rate and price-pegging measures can take the place of the spontaneous mechanism that in the past has been so successful in securing international trade equilibrium and the perennial nature of human communities.

How efficient, then, are the systems which at present throughout the world are intended to remedy the inadequacy of stabilizing mechanisms through a deliberate organization of international trade?

In the first instance, we have the example of the war. Naturally, during the hostilities, planning was relatively efficient. It was relatively easy to plan international trade because international trade, if any, was practically nonexistent. Transport was virtually under State control, frontiers were closed, and shipping space was allocated by the State. Imports required countless authorizations. It was thus possible to a considerable extent to plan international trade, and above all to limit imports to a level commensurate with foreign exchange availabilities which in turn were conditioned by political agreements on the allocation of credit.

In peace-time, however, the problem is completely different.

First, in time of peace one must find a foreign purchaser if one is to secure foreign exchange resources. You know better than I the problem of seeking a foreign purchaser, but you are also aware that up until now there are very few means of compelling a foreigner to make a purchase when he does not want to because the product offered him is too expensive in terms of his national currency. Save in exceptional periods when nothing is offered for sale, it is essentially on the basis of price considerations that purchases are made, but when the difference between domestic prices and foreign prices is the reverse of what it should be, the foreign purchaser does not buy. Hence the fact that, after having disrupted the foreign exchange mechanism, when one wants to sell abroad in spite of all that, one has to "intervene."

Relative prices have to be modified, by various equalization techniques or by direct subsidization. This is a common procedure in countries with planned economies. The price of the product intended for export must be lowered to the level at which a purchaser comes forward to buy it. But subsidies are costly; the resources that can be derived from exports secured by such means are inevitably limited. Imports must therefore be reduced to the level of availabilities. It should be noted that under a system of fixed foreign exchange rates, as there is at the same time a continuing deficit, domestic prices are continually rising. As a result, the situation is not stable and keeps deteriorating, and it becomes more and more difficult to find foreign purchasers, which means that it becomes more and more difficult to secure foreign exchange resources. Import restrictions must therefore be further intensified. This system thus inevitably tends to scale down to zero the amount of feasible imports, because the longer it lasts, the further the amount of resources derived from exports declines.

Where exports have become nil, then devaluation usually occurs. But the same process sets in again from the level that it generated. After a certain time, one finds again that the amount of resources available is nil; a further devaluation measure is then taken. One is therefore engaged in a planning system that, as you see, is governed by forces that are not particularly "deliberate."

We have to hand the example of our British neighbors. British economists tell us: "*We* know how to plan our balance of payments, we have self-discipline and public-spiritedness, and we have established an efficient system for the organization of international trade." Well, let us then have a look at what the British have done.

I recently received a document, *Economic Survey for 1948*,

which is extremely interesting. It sets forth the prospects and targets for 1948 and reviews the degree of fulfilment of the 1947 objectives.

One must pay a tribute to the British for their frankness and sincerity in reporting on their management results. I find on page 56 of this document Appendix I, which shows the degree to which the 1947 targets were fulfilled. I read the following:

	In million pounds sterling
Excess of expenditure on imports	124
Excess of Government expenditure abroad	36
Deficiency in receipts from exports and re-exports	75
Deficiency in net invisible income	90
TOTAL DEFICIT IN RELATION TO ESTIMATES	325

At present rates of exchange, 325 million pounds is the equivalent of more than 300,000 million French francs. One must admit that the efficiency of planning in this so-called ideal country for economic planning was fairly limited in 1947. Some will say that the situation is better in 1948. Let us await the results.

On the next page of the same document there is a piece of information which is more interesting still, perhaps because it is more simple: i.e., the effective distribution of manpower in Britain compared with estimates. One finds two columns, as follows:

MANPOWER DISTRIBUTION		
	As estimated in 1947 Survey	Actual
Coal industry	+ 40,000	+ 28,000
Public utilities (water, gas, electricity)	+ 17,000	+ 6,000
Transport and shipping	− 3,000	+ 54,000
Agriculture and fishing	+ 39,000	+ 9,000
Building and civil engineering	+ 50,000	+ 75,000

You can appreciate, gentlemen, how difficult it is in a country which is not a slave State—i.e., a country which does not practice the Hitlerite method of forced labor—to plan the distribution of labor. You are fully aware that under our political regimes, workers fortunately have the right to determine freely what use they make of their labor force and that they make the determination having regard in particular to the wage terms offered.

The British sensed the difficulty. A few months ago, they empowered their Government to require any worker to accept a given type of employment. They have thus moved toward compulsory distribution of manpower. As far as I am concerned, I am quite sure that this measure will be ineffective because Britain is too devoted to individual freedom for such a system, so akin to the slavery system, to be applied there. It is inconceivable that under our political regimes compulsory distribution of manpower could be a successful practice.

But if one cannot secure manpower distribution in conformity with plans, one will not succeed in fulfilling the objectives and one will therefore not be in a position to export those articles intended to be exported. One will therefore not have the foreign exchange availabilities deemed necessary to finance imports. Furthermore, in the absence of such foreign exchange availabilities, one will no doubt be obliged to come to an Import-Export system such as the one we mentioned earlier, because such a system will afford the only way of providing the foreign exchange necessary to enable you to say in production.

But there again, some will say: "You are a backward man, because that is national planning, whereas with the International Monetary Fund you have planning of the international type which is likely to ensure efficiently balance-of-payments equilibrium with no adverse effects from exchange rate and price movements."

Now, let us see see what international planning in fact amounts to.

In the Bretton Woods Agreements, which constitutes the charter for the International Monetary Fund, a number of chapters provide for economic organization measures. In the first place, it is stated that the par value of a member's currency as previously approved by the Fund must be maintained. When a change is proposed, concurrency by the Fund must be obtained. You will certainly remember that it was not so easy for us to secure concurrence by the Fund in our proposed new exchange system.

Article XX, Section 4 is particularly significant on account of its title—"Initial Determination of Par Values." Before going into operation, the Fund was to ask each prospective member State to communicate the par value of its currency that it intended to apply. The Fund was to concur in the proposed par value only after a thorough study that was to lead to a finding that the proposed par value was reasonable and likely to ensure balance-of-payments equilibrium.

What happened in fact? Each State communicated to the Fund the par value that happened to obtain at the time when the Fund was on the eve of beginning exchange transactions, and the Fund, after a few weeks of reflection, concurred in all existing par values.

As you can see, this is a fairly limited degree of planning. The Fund recognized that the problem of the *a priori* determination of the optimum par value of the currency of each country was such a complex problem implicating all factors related to internal equilibrium—wage levels, price levels, social structure—that it was inconceivable that such a small group of people without due authority, sitting in Washington, should resolve that here or there, in France, in Belgium, in Luxemburg, in the Netherlands, a Fund decision should result in the par value being altered.

As soon as the question arose of implementing Article XX, Section 4, it appeared that the responsibility vested in the Fund was purely theoretical and that the Fund could only do one thing, namely, concur in all the par values proposed by the States. I would very much like to be told what degree of international planning this represents. This is, of course, a semblance of planning, but has none of the realities.

It is true I must say, however, that there is another article in the Fund's Articles of Agreement—Article VII—which first mentions the situation that emerges when a general scarcity of a particular currency is developing . . . This is a situation with which we are quite familiar! Here the Fund has decisive functions . . . (Section 3[a]):

> *If it becomes evident to the Fund that the demand for a member's currency seriously threatens the Fund's ability to supply that currency, the Fund, whether or not it has issued a report under Section 1 of this Article, shall formally declare such currency scarce and shall thenceforth apportion its existing and accruing supply of the scarce currency with due regard to the relative needs of members, the general international economic situation, and any other pertinent considerations. The Fund shall also issue a report concerning its action.*

What will happen when the Fund publishes a report on the reasons underlying the dollar scarcity throughout the world? The report may be read, in limited circles. But will this change in any way domestic policies that are the resultant of the deep-lying—emotional rather than rational—tendencies that inspire peoples?

It is true that the founders of the Fund, who were wise and cautious, had intended to provide the Fund with a weapon that they thought decisive. It is the weapon afforded by Article XII, Section 8: "Communication of views to members":

> *The Fund shall at all times have the right to communicate its views informally to any member on any matter arising under this Agreement. The Fund may, by a two-thirds majority of the total voting power, decide to publish a report made to a member regarding its monetary or economic conditions and developments which directly tend to produce a serious disequilibrium in the international balance of payments of members.*

There is the ultimate weapon—publication of a report. If the Fund has views—and I have shown you that, up until now, it had not had any so far as the par values of the national currencies are concerned—it is provided with a decisive weapon, which is the possibility of publishing its views . . . Well, gentlemen, everything I have been telling you does show that when one claims to have substituted international planning for the action of self-acting spontaneous mechanisms, in the first place one has told an untruth, and this is regrettable, but above all one has laid oneself open to ridicule.

You know the wrist watches that young children wear. These watches have hands which move when you turn the winder, but there are no works inside. They bear a strange resemblance to the Bretton Woods instrument. The outward shape has been reproduced, but the inside has been surrendered. What you have is no longer an international trade regulating device, but a mere semblance of a device. And the planning which you claimed was to replace the foregone mechanism is, as I have shown you, a mere mockery.

What, then is the situation?

The situation is a very simple one. We have destroyed all the mechanisms that were likely to ensure international equilibrium. They have ceased to exist and have only been replaced by semblances of planning.

In such a context, it is not surprising that you should be unable to secure the necessary foreign exchange to buy your raw materials. It would indeed be surprising if you could.

However, it is essential that you should be able to import if you want the French people to be clad. If we really were living under a planning system, the relative importance of the various foreign currency requirements would have been weighed and import licenses would have been allocated to you accordingly.

But all those who have attempted to plan a balance of payments know that in this field reasoned action is not feasible. The problem is far too complex to be amenable to analytical methods . . . I recall a negotiation with a South American country. The question was to provide that country, as a result of our purchases, with the foreign exchange necessary for payment of the claims of our bond holders. We could buy copper, nitrate fertilizers, or onions. We were therefore faced with two possible alternatives: We could either reduce the outlets of certain metropolitan or colonial producers, or reduce the service that French lenders, who were the holders of claims on that country, would be receiving.

The problem was incredibly simple. Do you believe that it could be solved purposefully? And yet the problems that planners have to solve daily are infinitely more complicated, since instead of having to choose between four solutions only, they are confronted with anything between 10,000 and 100,-000 possible alternatives, all equally feasible.

Some say that I once dealt with mathematical problems at the Polytechnic School. As I remember it, if a problem is to be solved by mathematical analysis, it must not be unduly complicated. The moment you are confronted with systems having four or five unknown quantities, the most talented human brain is left powerless. What about systems with an infinity of unknown quantities?[1] Yet you have to make up your mind. If you are dishonest, you will rely on selfish criteria connected with political or financial interests. But if you are honest, you do as your friends in the Finance Ministry did toward you: You select an arbitrary criterion, telling yourself that this is not a reasoned solution, that it may not even be a reasonable solution, but that all the same it *is* a solution.

Thus it is that under the Import-Export system you have been authorized to retain your foreign exchange earnings and to use them as best you think. But what are the implications of such a decision?

It places in the hands of those who purchase your products—that is, foreigners—the determination of what quantities of wool will be available to the French people. Depending on whether those foreigners buy more or less, the French will have more or less fabric to clothe themselves. Now, the moment you have had a devaluation the internal process is always the same. Domestic prices increase, which means that your outlets are gradually whittled down. Hence the fact that the wool available for domestic consumption will gradually

[1] At the time of this lecture, ordinators were not yet in current use.

decline in quantity until a further devaluation opens up new outlets for you. Can one really call this planning? It is arbitrariness pure and simple. I would even say that the only advantage, the only merit of the system which is being applied to you is that it is arbitrary. It bears out the fact that those who devised it wanted to restore some degree of automatism, i.e., to free themselves from having to choose on the basis of interests that they knew they could not decide between, at least not in a way that they could publicly own. A tragic thing in the world that we have created is that, in the circumstances in which we live, one cannot conceive of a better solution. I do not think there is one. We have built up a preposterous world and we are bearing the burden of this absurdity.

But then, what does the future hold in store for us?

I am convinced that we can choose between two systems, but not more than two.

I would not wish you to infer from my remarks that planning is necessarily inefficient. I do not think so. On the contrary, I am of the opinion that when certain requirements are met, planning can have a certain degree of efficiency. During the last war, the Germans did succeed in establishing a kind of planning that was not fully efficient, but which was more efficient than the one that we are attempting to follow. I think that the Russians have succeeded in carrying out their five-year plans with some degree of precision. But planning can be efficient only if it is supported by concentration camps, informing, postal censorship, spying, the reduction to the minimum of benefits conferred on individuals—so many things that we were all familiar with during the occupation.

If all this is wanted, then planning may afford a solution.

But if you are abhorrent to it—and I do hope that there are in the world a number of men who are—then one must state and proclaim that there is only one way out—I say so with the certainty that I am right, with all the conviction that I can command—and that is to restore, and to restore as promptly as possible, the mechanisms likely to ensure automatically equilibrium in balances of payments without total planning based on concentration camps.

What is the policy that can yield such a result? There again, I believe that there is no need to hesitate over the choice. The ultimate goal is convertibility. But convertibility cannot be restored overnight when domestic budgets are in deficit, the more so as the rate at which it is to be re-established would not be known. The optimum rate of exchange must be determined, and that is a very difficult problem which I have had to solve three times in my past career.

In 1926, I was called to Premier Poincaré's Cabinet to draw up a memorandum on the franc stabilization rate. In 1927, I was called upon to do the same in Greece, then in 1928 in Bulgaria. The determination of the optimum exchange rate is one of the most difficult problems because it involves an infinity of solutions that bring into play all the elements of the domestic situation.

In particular, it requires a decision as to the level at which wages will be allowed to settle.

In Poincaré's days, our basic criterion was the need to select a rate that would involve no wage reduction. This floor was a basic "must." As far as the ceiling was concerned, it hinges on the fiscal policy that the government is able and willing to apply. The yield of a given fiscal system is not a specific problem. It depends on the efforts that the country is prepared to make and the authority with which the government can impose them. It is therefore not possible *a priori* to come out in favor of a given rate rather than another. Public opinion must be sounded out and the national determination to put matters on a sound basis and to accept sacrifices must be assessed. And this is not something that can be done in all certainty in each and every case.

I am convinced that this convertibility problem is in fact the problem of civilization in the world. Depending on whether or not you move toward convertibility, you will or will not tend to restore what we used to call "civilization." Ethics, the binding nature of commitments entered into, justice, individual responsibility—all these are notions that have no meaning in a system which, by denying you the necessary foreign exchange, makes it impossible for you to settle your debts. Under foreign exchange controls, there can be no such thing as individual responsibility. There can be no individual responsibility for an industrialist whose fate depends on the coal quota allocated to him.

The entire future of our civilization depends on what decisions we shall take in the field of monetary policy. The situation is serious because the evil is deep-rooted.

I do not believe that all the problems arising from the deterioration of the present system of international trade could be remedied by anything other than an overall solution, setting forth clearly the objective to be reached and giving it precedence over all other problems.

If such a solution is to be feasible, it must be agreed to by all those whose thought and life are bound up with monetary problems.

It sometimes happens that we look at the world so closely that the general picture escapes us.

These reflections lead me to the conclusion that, with the system that we have established, there is no longer any reason why balances of payments should be in equilibrium.

If this is conceded, then all men of good faith, whatever party they belong to, whatever their ulterior motives may be, should agree on this basic requirement that a system that can not only endure but even exist should be restored in the world as soon as possible. I for one am convinced that if such a system is really wanted, failing the eventuality of total planning, there is no other solution than to revert at the earliest possible moment to a metal convertibility system.

Let me make one final essential remark on the social implications of this conclusion. People often say: "This is a ruthless system, it imposes sufferings on the most underprivileged classes." A little while ago, your President was speaking of the articles which I published recently in *Le Figaro:* In the parliamentary debate, a French deputy said: "In those articles Mr. Rueff proposes the lifting of price controls and the pegging of wages; it is therefore on the poverty of the people that he bases the restoration of a sound situation."

I did not give him the lie, because all those who had read my articles know that the contention attributed to me was not in fact mine.

The question was in no way one of pegging wages and lifting price controls, but only of making headway toward mobility of both prices and wages in order to make it possible for the French people to acquire the maximum amount of products and therefore the maximum amount of welfare.

Within the framework of a free price and free convertibility policy, there is no obstacle in the way of a generous social policy. But if such a policy is not to jeopardize the stability of the general price level, it must be implemented within the framework of a balanced budget, which means that you must "rob Peter to pay Paul."

A free price policy is not an antisocial policy. On the contrary, it is the only policy that can really provide the most underprivileged classes with those benefits that they are entitled to expect and that contrary policies always promise but never produce.

As regards programs for widening the market and instituting Customs unions—which are so often mentioned but are so meaningless in view of the present status of international trade—there is only one way of implementing them: and that is to restore an international monetary system that can ensure equilibrium in balance of payments at all times, thereby making it possible to eliminate trade obstacles in the international community that it is intended to set up.

4

THE 1928 PROBLEM,

FOCUSING ON GERMAN

REPARATIONS

A. An Economic Error: the
Organization of Transfers[1]

Balance-of-payments equilibrium

Under one of the most original provisions of the Dawes Plan, a Committee on Transfers was entrusted with the task of ensuring that no payments in cash was made by Germany if it threatened to impair the stability of the mark.

This provision is of course based on the idea that the amount of monies that can be transferred without generating monetary disturbances is strictly limited and might in particular be less than the aggregate amounts levied by Germany, directly or indirectly, on its domestic economy in order to meet the reparations burden.

Furthermore, the setting up of the Committee on Transfers is not the only element that demonstrates that such an

[1] This study was published in *L'Information*, November 4, 7, and 8, 1928, and in pamphlet form in the same year by Gaston Doin et Cie, publishers (out of print).

idea is very widely accepted; resort to payments in kind also implies belief in a limitation of the amount of the yearly installment transferable in cash.

This chapter is devoted to an examination of the contention that, in given economic circumstances, it may not be possible to transfer abroad the totality of the domestic currency availabilities derived from fiscal levies. Its practical purpose cannot be doubted, since it tends to determine whether the extent to which transfers can be effected can justifiably be adduced in support of a limitation of the yearly installments that debtor countries have to pay.

The study will deliberately neglect the political aspects of the problem and limit itself to the economic issues involved. Thus, all the factual considerations on which expert recommendations may have been based in 1924 will not be mentioned here, nor will the indirect guarantees that at that time may have resulted from their implementation. While, therefore, we claim that the organization of transfers is an economic error, this view is not held in relation to the specific problem which the Dawes Committee experts had to resolve in 1924—it may in fact be that the setting up of a Committee on Transfers was at the time the expedient best suited to the complex political situation which it was intended to resolve —but only in relation to the economic contentions that such organization seems to imply and which, in fact, public opinion believed to be supported by the experts.

THE THEORY OF TRANSFERS

The belief that there is a transfer problem stems from the idea that at every point of time the balance of the external debit and credit items of a country is determined with a certain degree of precision by quasi-permanent economic factors.

If one were to admit that this is indeed the case, the introduction into the balance of payments of the country concerned of a new major debit item—such as the one resulting for Germany from its reparations burden—would threaten to disrupt the equilibrium of that balance of payments, failing an offsetting item in the form of foreign claims payable on demand. By not abstaining from making the transfers which this new debit item involves, one would inevitably cause, where the currency was not stabilized, continuing depreciation of the currency of the debtor country, and, where the currency was stabilized, the gradual depletion of the gold or foreign exchange reserves that make it possible to maintain monetary stability. In both cases, by not suspending immediately the foreign payments that had generated these disturbances, one would inevitably cause serious disruption and probably irreparable catastrophes in the economy of the debtor country. It would appear that the Committee on Transfers was created and duly empowered to suspend any foreign payments that might jeopardize the stability of the German currency in order to avoid such disruptions.

THE EQUILIBRIUM OF INTERNATIONAL SETTLEMENTS BEFORE THE WAR

The moment one attempts to assess the usefulness, in the postwar international organization, of the newly created Committee on Transfers, one cannot fail to recognize that prior to its establishment, and although international trade was particularly buoyant, no catastrophe of the type that it was intended to avoid ever occurred.

Indeed, before the war, external debts were freely incurred everywhere in the world for the most varied reasons and without any kind of controls, whereas capital movements —loans to governments or private individuals—caused considerable and abrupt variations in balances of payments. However, in such circumstances, when the conditions for equilibrium of balances of payments were constantly changing, in no case were the reserves of a Bank of Issue ever fully exhausted.

What is more, the residual gold movements from country to country were always extremely limited in relation to the volume of international trade, without any Committee on Transfers or, for that matter, any other body ever having to limit the amount of foreign commitments to the amount of foreign claims payable on demand.

It is therefore clear beyond any doubt that the equilibrium that the Committee on Transfers has been responsible for maintaining since 1924 in favor of Germany was practically secured in a continuing way in every country before the war. Now, such equilibrium resulted from the simultaneous behavior of all individuals who freely contributed, directly or otherwise, to the emergence of international commitments. May I call attention to the fact that any person who, in France, drinks tea, eats chocolate, wears cotton socks or a jacket made of English cloth, consumes petrol in his car, or buys Rio Tinto or de Beers shares in London introduces a debit item into the French balance of payments; similarly, that any Englishman, Brazilian, or Japanese who drinks a bottle of burgundy or champagne, buys a French book or a trinket made in France introduces a credit item into the French balance of payments. This means that, in practice, the sum total of the daily actions of millions and millions of individuals throughout the world contributes to the formation at every point of time of what we call in economic jargon the debit and credit sides of the French balance-of-payments ledger.

Now, these countless individuals act in all freedom in a totally unrelated manner from one another. Each is entirely ignorant of what the others are doing, and at no time does any of them worry about the effects of his actions on the balance of international commitments. That the sum total of these individual transactions should, in a permanent way and in respect of every country, bring about the marvelous equilibrium that is reflected in the small amount of gold moving throughout the world is indeed an extremely curious fact and one that can in no way be attributed to chance.

Indeed, if there were no relationship whatsoever between the aggregate amount of the external debts of a country and its total foreign claims, one could agree that it might happen once, as a result of truly extraordinary circumstances, that the amount of the former might roughly equal the amount of the latter. But it would be just as impossible that this should be the case always and in every place, as a result of the action of 100 or 200 million individuals acting in a totally unrelated manner, as to imagine, to use M. Emile Borel's well-known simile, that monkeys let loose in a typewriter shop could reproduce all the books in the British Museum by banging away at random on the keyboards.

But if this cannot be a chance equilibrium, since it does in fact exist, the reason must be that there is in the economic order one cause that brings it about; and this cause can only be the functioning of a mechanism which at every point of time balances the external debts and external claims of the various countries with a degree of accuracy that is reflected in the order of magnitude of gold movements in relation to the volume of international trade.

Some will observe, of course, that this mechanism could operate normally before the war when fairly stable trade flows had slowly been adjusted to quasi-permanent economic circumstances, but that in a perturbed period such as was the case after the signature of the peace treaties, natural phenomena would fail to maintain equilibrium in balances of payments, above all when equilibrium was disrupted by such artificial commitments as war reparations debts, the amount of which has moreover been constantly changing, at least during the period when the Dawes Plan operated.

A cursory look at prewar statistics provides an easy answer to such comments. At the time, trade flows were not at all stable and year-to-year variations in the amount of commercial debts often exceeded the variations in annual installments under the Dawes Plan during their growth period.

Thus, French merchandise imports increased from 5,640 million to 6,240 million francs from 1908 to 1909, representing a difference of 600 million prewar francs. If the value of exports had remained unchanged, serious disturbances might have ensued. But precisely, although there was no Committee on Transfers in existence, nor any body entrusted with the task of equating the amount of foreign claims with the amount of foreign debts, the value of exports increased by

668 million francs—from 5,050 million to 5,718 million francs—during the same period, thereby offsetting the debt surplus resulting from the increase in imports.[1]

And since no catastrophe of the kind that the Dawes experts had feared for Germany ever took place, this adjustment was not an exceptional fact occurring in a particular period and in a given country, but one that happened all the time and in all countries with unfailing regularity.

Thus, we must admit that before the war there did exist a mechanism—which did not in any way threaten the monetary health of the various States—that equated the amount of their external claims with the amount of their foreign debts at every point of time, regardless of the velocity of variations in the amount of such international commitments. This mechanism automatically brought about equilibrium in balances of payments and thus fulfilled the functions which, so far as Germany is concerned, have been vested in the Committee on Transfers since 1924.

There remains of course to assess the efficiency of its action. It might indeed be that in exceptionally adverse circumstances such as those in which Germany would be under the Dawes system, it might generate a tendency toward the restoration of equilibrium, but that this tendency by itself would not suffice to secure such equilibrium.

THE FRENCH TRADE BALANCE
SINCE 1914

To appreciate this point, the best way is to study the changes which have occurred in the French trade balance since 1914.

According to French Customs statistical returns, imports exceeded exports by 1,518 million francs in 1912 and 1,540 million francs in 1914. According to the views expressed

[1] It would have been just as appropriate to consider the increase in exports as the initial phenomenon. In addition, it should be borne in mind that equilibrium can be restored by variations in invisible items, as happens most of the time. But this aspect is neglected here for the sake of simplification.

above, if during those periods the balance of payments was necessarily in equilibrium, the reason was that in the invisible sector credit items exceeded debit items by about 1,500 million francs.[1]

These invisible items include all the international claims or debts that do not appear in the Customs returns and arise essentially out of capital movements, income from foreign securities, maritime transport operations for foreign account, banking operations, or catering for foreign tourists . . . Before the war, the general consensus was that income from foreign securities held by French nationals was an important credit item in the French balance of payments.

There is no doubt that during the war the value of this declined considerably. An important part of the foreign securities portfolio held by French people was handed over to the State at the Government's request and was sold by the State in order to secure foreign currency resources. In addition, certain securities which French people held in considerable quantity—such as Russian bonds—have become unproductive. It is therefore obvious that if after the war the other French balance-of-payments items—in particular the trade balance—had remained unchanged compared with 1913, the French balance of accounts would have shown a deficit. If equilibrium was to be maintained, it was necessary that a diminution in the external debit item should offset the diminution in credit items resulting from the elimination in the balance-of-payments assets of a notable part of French income from abroad.

In 1921 and 1922 there was no inflow of foreign tourists into France as in subsequent years. Furthermore, the considerable capital export movement that was recorded in subsequent years had not yet commenced. Conditions were therefore hardly different from what they had been before the war, and a diminution in external debit items could result only from a reduction of the trade deficit.

This being the case, it can be noted that in 1921—still

[1] We are using the same arguments again. But in 1928 they were just as essential to the demonstration as in 1949 or in 1965.

according to the monthly returns of the Customs Department
—the French trade balance showed a 2,295 million franc deficit. These were, of course, paper francs which cannot be compared with prewar francs. If the 1921 and 1913 deficits are to
be compared, they should be expressed in one single unit
such as the dollar, for instance.

In 1913, the French trade deficit, expressed in dollars, was
1,540:5.18, i.e., 297 million dollars. During 1921 the average
exchange rate was 13.49 French francs to the dollar. In the
same year, therefore, the French trade deficit amounted to
2,295:13.49, i.e., 170 million dollars, representing approximately 57 per cent of the 1913 deficit.

One would arrive at a similar result for 1922.

Thus, in 1921 and 1922, the French trade deficit was reduced to about one-half its 1913 figure.[1]

In order to appreciate the significance of this finding, one
should bear in mind the situation in France in 1921 and 1922.
At that time, the most productive part of the national territory was practically idle; on the other hand, domestic needs
were in excess of anything that could have been imagined
before the war, both for the reconstruction of war-devastated
areas and for the rehabilitation of the country that had been
exhausted by the war. And it was in these extremely unfavorable circumstances, at a time when most industries were
unable to export and imports were unrestricted, that the
French trade deficit fell to half its prewar level. Furthermore,
this result was achieved without any kind of intervention,
without any import control committee, without any artificial
export incentives, at a time when it seemed quite impossible
to attain it. It is precisely because such a phenomenon is so
hard to believe that it should evidence the irresistible power
of the mechanism that generated it, a mechanism that, in the
most unfavorable circumstances, achieved what no human
intervention could ever hope to do.

[1] In subsequent years, when mass capital exports introduced new debit
items into the French balance of payments, the French trade deficit declined
further and even turned into a surplus. This is again a fact worth noting,
the analysis of which would lead to the same conclusions.

Prices and international
payments equilibrium

In the preceding chapter we have shown the existence and the power of the mechanism which secures and maintains balance-of-payments equilibrium between nations, without any authoritative intervention. In order to make more obvious still the uselessness of an organization intended to protect debtor countries, in particular Germany, against the alleged risks inherent in transfers, there only remains to show what is precisely the nature of this mechanism.

To that effect, we shall study, as an illustration, the problem that arose when our allies suddenly decided, early in 1919, to cease granting those credits which were enabling France to maintain its balance-of-payments equilibrium.

In both 1917 and 1918, the credits that Britain and the United States extended to France for political reasons amounted to more than 17,000 million francs, not including commercial credits. These foreign credits, which were entered as income in the French balance of payments, vanished overnight, thus leaving an annual gap of about 17,000 million francs—practically the equivalent of so many prewar francs. The situation was therefore quite similar to that which would have resulted from the sudden introduction into the French balance of payments of a debit item of the same amount, such as for instance a reparations debt. Strictly speaking, the problem that arose was therefore a transfer problem whose magnitude, however, was quite exceptional and far greater than that of all the problems arising out of the payment of reparations by Germany.

To determine how the problem was solved, one must first recall the classical theory, which contends that balance-of-payments equilibrium is strictly ensured at every point of time by exchange or price movements. According to this theory, whenever a balance of payments is in deficit, there occurs, under the influence of the transfers of purchasing power that generated the deficit and of the resulting gold movements, a decline in domestic prices and a rise in the exchange rates of foreign currencies that tend to stimulate exports and reduce imports until the previously existing equilibrium is restored.

In this simplified formulation, the classical theory calls for many reservations; however, as we have shown in our book on the "Theory of Monetary Phenomena" ("Théorie des phénomènes monétaires"),[2] they can be overlooked here without impairing the analysis of the problem.

Thus, in order to determine whether the phenomena which classical theory allows one to expect did in fact occur when the French balance of payments showed a deficit as a result of the elimination of international credits, we shall compare the general price level in France with the general level of prices in other countries, expressed in francs, the latter level being the average British and United States price levels valued in francs.

The level of American prices, expressed in francs, will represent what Frenchmen would have had to pay to purchase, during the period under consideration, the assortment of goods used for the determination of the United States wholesale price index, the price of this assortment being assumed equal to 100 in the year 1913, selected as the base year. Thus, whenever the French level of prices exceeds the average level of foreign prices, expressed in francs, it would be more profitable on account of the price differential to make purchases abroad and to sell in France; French imports will thereby be stimulated and exports will be discouraged. Conversely, whenever this difference is reduced and whenever it is reduced to the point of becoming negative, it will be profitable to purchase in France and sell abroad, since the French price level will be less than the foreign price level expressed in francs. French exports will thus be stimulated and French imports hampered, and the greater in absolute terms the minus differential, the greater this twofold effect will be.

2 Payot, publishers, 1927, Part II (out of print).

If therefore the classical theory is right, then whenever the balance of payments of a given country shows a sudden deficit, *one should be able to perceive a sudden decline* in the difference between the domestic price level and the level of foreign prices expressed in the national currency of the country concerned, and this narrowing down should continue as long as the deficit is maintained and disappear only when the previously existing equilibrium has been restored.

THE EXAMPLE OF FRANCE FROM 1919 TO 1922

In order to see whether the above views are correct, let us consider what happened when the French balance of payments showed a deficit as a result of the sudden disappearance of international credits that were serving to maintain its equilibrium.

The chart on page 93 shows the variations in the difference between the French price level and the average level of foreign prices, expressed in francs, during the period 1915–22. The lower chart (dotted line) shows the variations in the French trade balance during the same period.

Thus, it can be noted that in 1917 and 1918 the French trade balance shows a deficit of approximately 20,000 million francs per year. But the deficit is fully met by political credits, in a roughly equivalent amount, granted us by our allies. At no time, therefore, is there in the foreign exchange market any unsatisfied demand for foreign currencies against French francs; everything takes place as if the French balance of payments was in equilibrium.

Furthermore, throughout this period the rate of exchange for foreign currencies is determined artificially as a result of those foreign credits, and, as the price level rises faster in France than in other countries, the difference between the French price level and the level of foreign prices expressed in francs increases. Far from contributing to restore equilibrium in the trade balance, this difference tends to stimulate imports and limit exports—which in no way con-

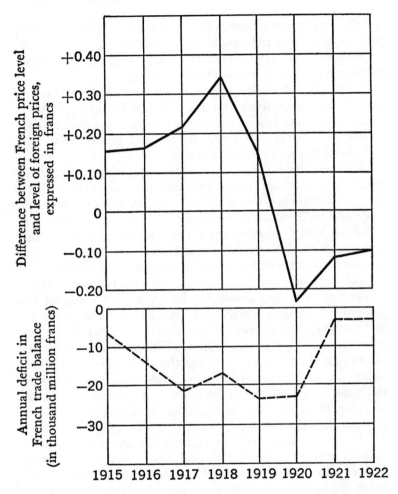

Difference between French price level and level of foreign prices, expressed in francs.

flicts with theory since the balance of payments is in equilibrium.

But in the first quarter of 1919, our allies ceased granting us the credits that were enabling us to offset our trade deficit. A sudden gap—approximately 17,000 million francs per year—appears in the French balance of payments.

Our charts show that from then on the difference between the French price level and the level of foreign prices expressed in francs begins to decline and that the decline continues so long as the trade deficit, and consequently the balance-of-payments deficit, persists.

In 1920 the difference becomes a negative one, and its magnitude is exceptional. From that time onward, it therefore constitutes an extremely powerful export incentive and a considerable hindrance to exports. From that time onward, but from that time only, the trade deficit begins to decline, concurrently with the difference between the French price level and the level of foreign prices expressed in francs.

In 1921, the deficit falls to approximately 2,000 million francs per year, i.e., about one-half the gold value of the corresponding 1913 figure, and since there do not exist yet any major capital export movements, there is no doubt that the balance of payments is in equilibrium. The difference ceases recording any variations at the same time as the trade balance, and the average values of both will remain substantially the same until such time as there appears in the balance of payments a new deficit engendered by major capital exports in the subsequent period.

A mere look at the above charts, the fact that the trade deficit did not start to decline until 1921 when the difference between the French price level and the level of foreign prices expressed in francs had reached a considerable negative figure and not, as might have been expected, directly after the war, that is in 1919 or 1920, together with the many examples that can be found in similar circumstances and the considerations previously adduced—shows that there cannot be the slightest doubt as to the influence of variations in the difference between the French price levels and the level of foreign prices, expressed in francs, on the restoration of equilibrium in the French balance of payments.

Furthermore, the nature of the mechanism accounts for the fact that it succeeded in restoring equilibrium in the most unfavorable circumstances imaginable. Indeed, it is bound to be irresistible since the decline in the difference between the French price level and the level of foreign prices expressed in francs continues so long as the generating cause has not been fully eliminated, i.e., so long as the balance-of-payments deficit persists. This accounts for the fact that nothing can prevent the restoration or the maintenance of equilibrium in balances of payments, not even the highest tariffs.

MONETARY DEPRECIATION

Some will say, however, that equilibrium was safely restored only at the cost of a particularly serious monetary depreciation, whereas what must be primarily avoided is monetary disturbances.

Now, the above charts show precisely that monetary depreciation is in no way necessary to the unfolding of the restoration-of-equilibrium process. What does in fact bring about the restoration of equilibrium is not the rise in foreign exchange rates, but the decline in the level of domestic prices relative to the level of foreign prices expressed in francs.

This decline can be the result of either a decline in French prices or a rise in the exchange rates of foreign currencies expressed in francs. If this decline is to occur in a period when the level of French prices increases faster than the level of foreign prices, then the rate of exchange of foreign currencies must increase, first to offset internal depreciation of the national currency and, in the second instance, to generate, as between the level of French prices and the level of foreign prices expressed in francs, the difference that will bring about the restoration of equilibrium.

And what is precisely noteworthy in the facts observed in 1919 is that all those variations that one might have thought to be fortuitous or disorderly were in fact such as to cause the movement of exchange rates first to offset the price movement and then to generate the phenomenon which theory commanded should occur.

But if, at the time, the rate of exchange had been stabilized, then the same variation between the level of domestic prices and the level of foreign prices expressed in French francs might have occurred as a result of a mere price decline in France. A comprehensive theory of this phenomenon should indicate that this price decline invariably results from the transfer of purchasing power subsequently upon the deficit, but the limited length of the present chapter does not permit us to dwell on this point here. Furthermore, our only purpose here is to show that monetary depreciation is in no way a prerequisite to the solution of a transfer problem. On the contrary, such a solution can be reached in a better way and more easily in a period of monetary stability than under a system of fluctuating exchange rates and without anything, in the phenomena which bring about the restoration of equilibrium, being likely to jeopardize the stability of the national currency.[1]

THE BUDGET ASPECT

In order fully to justify the application of this theory to reparations payments, one last objection must be met. Some will say that monetary phenomena cannot generate the export surplus which will restore balance-of-payments equilibrium unless German production can yield an exportable surplus equal in value to the amount of foreign payments that has to be offset.

And this is precisely where the reserve formulated earlier comes in; it will be remembered that we did not claim that any amount could be transferred without any monetary difficulty, but only that this was possible for an amount equal to the amount of revenue levied in Germany with a view to external payments. And if this is in fact the case, the reason is

[1] This gives one a foretaste of the aggregate demand theory which will be expounded in the second part of this book.

precisely that the effect of such a fiscal levy is only to with-draw from consumption in Germany the counterpart of those monies which are to be exported, thereby creating a surplus of wealth produced, but not consumed, in Germany that rep-resents a value strictly equal to that of the goods whose ex-port will be ensured by the unfolding of the monetary phe-nomena subsequent upon the transfer. It must be emphasized that this export surplus would not be generated if the State floated loans in foreign countries in order to secure the neces-sary resources for the settlement of its external payments; but then the surplus would no longer be necessary, since the foreign loan would provide directly the amount of foreign exchange necessary for its transfer to the creditor States.

Germany's payments capacity is limited only by its budget resources

The theoretical considerations that we have adduced to demonstrate that, contrary to an unduly widespread opinion, there was no real obstacle to the transfer outside Germany of the amount of revenue levied on the German economy will no doubt sound futile to practical people whose only concern is to construct a permanent mechanism intended to secure the transfer of all transferable monies without damaging the German currency.

In this respect, the transfer organization set up under the Dawes Plan has fulfilled the expectations of all our experts, since it freed them—so they believed—from having to form an opinion of their own on the nature and efficiency of the phenomenon that they were going to set in motion. Germany had to make payments abroad. They, the monetary experts, did not know to what extent it could do so without damaging the German currency, and they had only limited faith in the theories taught them. Never mind that: *experientia docet*. A Committee would be entrusted with the task of equating, at every point of time, the amount of effective transfers with current transfer possibilities.

THE ABSENCE OF A TRANSFER PROBLEM

Unfortunately, however, this formula, though apparently based on a spirit of realism, is absolutely meaningless. *In point of fact, transfer possibilities existing at a given moment cannot possibly limit the amount of transfers to be effected, since transfer possibilities precisely materialize at every point of time into actual transfers.* In these circumstances, suspension of a transfer on the grounds that one does not find in the exchange market the means necessary for effecting it simply amounts to a deliberate renunciation of the only measure that can make it feasible.

If an Expert Committee had been convened in 1919 to determine whether or not our allies could suspend the credits that they were granting us without damaging the French currency, it would undoubtedly have given a negative answer or would at least have laid down a plan for a progressive scaling down, so as at every point of time to equate the amount of credits granted with what our experts would have called the French balance-of-payments requirements. Thus, the trade deficit would, at every point of time, have declined only to the extent that the amount of credits granted had been reduced; France would have continued to incur foreign debts and the experts would have made her give up the only measure that could have brought about—and in fact did bring about—the restoration of equilibrium in its balance of payments.

Thus, wherever there is a transfer problem, it is the emergence of an imbalance in the balance of payments that places at the disposal of the debtor country the means that will enable it to pay its debt; any desire to avoid such loss of equilibrium amounts to a straightforward renunciation of the only factual occurrence that could make the transfer possible.

Hence the considerable danger for us of an organization whose task it is to equate German payments with transfer possibilities that such payments alone can generate and whose action, if strictly exerted, should in fact make such transfers impossible.[1]

THE IMPORTANCE OF THE
BUDGET PROBLEM

Furthermore, anyone conversant with the mechanism that ensures and maintains balance-of-payments equilibrium will realize that one cannot in any way adduce transfer considerations in support of a limitation of the annual instalments that Germany has to pay. The important thing is not to know what amounts Germany will be able to transfer—because Germany will be in a position to transfer all the monies that it has accumulated in marks in order to meet its reparations payments—but to know to what extent Germany will be able to increase its direct or indirect fiscal levies with a view to such payments. *The problem is therefore not a transfer problem, but a budget problem,* and the great merit of the Dawes Plan is that it has dealt with considerable strictness with that aspect of the problem and has ensured that reparations payments would in no way be likely to put the German budget in deficit.

PAYMENTS IN KIND

There is one last consequence that arises out of the views previously expressed; it concerns the institution of payments in kind.

Systematic resort to the transfer of goods from the debtor State to the creditor State directly generates an increase in exports that by itself may make it possible to discharge external commitments. From the monetary point of view, it therefore has the same effect as transfers in cash and does not in this respect present any advantage over the latter modality.

1 One cannot in any way consider as transfer experience the cash payments already made. The means of payments that made them possible were only yielded by a foreign loans surplus, so that until now there has been no real experience of transfers as they should occur under a permanent system.

On the other hand, it carries a great many particularly serious disadvantages.

In the first instance, by systematically channeling the exports of the debtor country toward the creditor country, it prevents any spontaneous redistribution—i.e., redistribution in conformity with the economic conditions obtaining at the particular point of time—of the export surplus that inevitably occurs in the balance of payments of the debtor country. It is indeed in no way indispensable that the creditor country should take up directly the goods exported by the debtor country. Such goods must be distributed throughout the world, in response to everybody's needs. Under the new state of equilibrium that would thus be established, the States that have taken up German exports without receiving transfers in cash will find that their own exports increase by a corresponding amount, so that the balances of payments of the creditor States alone will show an increase that is not offset by any corresponding item on the debit side.

But there is more: In order to be able to absorb payments in kind which it believes it is profitable to receive, the creditor State is induced to accept considerable sacrifices as far as the selling prices are concerned. It thus considerably reduces the profits that it derives from its debtor's payments, while laying open its own industry to extremely damaging competition which is both unjustified and unnecessary.

Last but not least, the creditor State not only sells the goods that it receives, but also wants to use them directly to the greatest extent possible. It is thus induced to undertake major public works schemes that, while of course not unnecessary, could have been postponed, and to incur considerable internal expenditures in order to carry them out.

The creditor State thus gives up all idea of using the payments made by the debtor country for their only legitimate purpose—the amortization of debts incurred in order to advance payment thereof—and instead, at a time when the most drastic measures of economy are of the essence, it writes into its budget items of expenditure which are not absolutely essential or which it might have deferred until some later date.

For all the above reasons, we are of the opinion that the institution of payments in kind would be justifiable only to the extent that it was truly indispensable. On the contrary, we have shown that this would in no way increase the amount of feasible transfers and would only result in reducing *ipso facto* the amount of monies which could be transferred in cash.

THE FINAL SETTLEMENT OF REPARATIONS

Thus a rational arrangement to solve the reparations problem should provide only for a mechanism of payments in cash, without any provision designed to solve the transfer problem. The latter, we are fully convinced, does not and cannot arise so long as the amounts to be transferred do not exceed the amount of budget revenue levied on the income of the debtor country.

Mr. Keynes' Views on the Transfer Problem

In the *Economic Journal* for March 1929, there appeared an article by Mr. Keynes, "The German Transfer Problem." In this article, Mr. Keynes answers those writers who believe that the transfer problem does not arise when budgetary problems have been solved, and that it may even be dangerous to provide machinery to maintain the equilibrium of the balance of payments of the debtor country.

Article published in French in *Revue d'Economie politique*, No. 4, 1929, and in English in the *Economic Journal*, September 1929.

In this study, we shall endeavor to summarize the British economist's arguments and to evaluate their scope.

In Mr. Keynes' criticism of the standpoint of the writers who deny the existence of a transfer problem, there are two fundamental observations, differing greatly both in character and in their respective consequences.

In the first, Mr. Keynes shows that, in his view, the settlement of reparations due from Germany raises not only a budget problem, but also a transfer problem, because "the expenditure of the German people must be reduced, *not only* by the amount of the reparation taxes which they must pay out of their earnings, but also by a reduction in their gold-rate of earnings below what they would otherwise be . . .

"The transfer problem consists in reducing the gold-rate of efficiency—earnings of the German factors of production sufficiently to enable them to increase their exports to an adequate aggregate total; the budgetary problem consists in extracting out of these reduced money-earnings a sufficient amount of reparation taxes."

On this point Mr. Keynes' assertion appears to be indisputable. But it is equally so when he says: "The reduction in real wages would be by no means so large as the reduction in money-wages, since the prices of home goods for home consumption might be expected to fall."

This seems to us an essential point. If it were possible to examine here the question from the point of view of economic theory by inquiring how equilibrium is maintained or restored, provisionally ignoring the resistances that in practice paralyze the play of economic phenomena, it could be shown that exchange and price movements—in other words, the movements of gold prices—that tend to maintain the equilibrium of a balance of payments, or restore it when it has been accidentally disturbed, affect equally all internal prices.

This is evident when, during a regime of forced currency, a variation in gold prices is brought about by means of a variation in the rate of foreign currencies reckoned in the national currency. In the case of metallic circulation, the proof is more complicated and constitutes a special aspect of the theory of prices; but we are sure that Mr. Keynes knows the result and does not dispute it. Assuming then that, in the adjustment which restores equilibrium to the balance of payments all the prices vary in the same proportion as wages, real wages are not modified. Hence, the purchasing power of the population remains unchanged, and the fall in gold prices which restored the equilibrium of the balance of accounts has imposed no new sacrifice on the population and has not altered its position in any way. As, moreover, this movement of prices is entirely spontaneous, we consider that it can be altogether ignored. It was for this reason that we felt justified in asserting that there was no transfer problem.

On the contrary, the levy that is to produce the necessary funds for the purchase of the exchange to be remitted to the foreign creditor will cause no fall in prices, since the purchasing power of which the population has been deprived will be transferred to the sellers of foreign exchange and utilized by them. As a result of this levy, there will therefore be a real decrease in the resources of the population of the debtor State, and this decrease, measured in purchasing power, will be exactly equal to the increase in the resources of the population of the creditor State.

The foregoing conclusions can also be deduced from a principle that I have always found confirmed in the various individual cases I have had to study. I should be astonished if Mr. Keynes had not, like myself, had occasion to enunciate this conclusion and if he did not admit its general applicability. This principle, which might be called the principle of the conservation of purchasing power, simply states that never in the course of the various economic transformations that occur is purchasing power lost or created, but that it always remains constant. The result is that in all cases one man's loss is another man's gain, as was very clearly shown by the levies made upon the holders of fixed income securities during the various inflation crises which followed the war. In the case before us, the principle of the conservation of purchasing power makes it possible to assert that, whatever the appearances may be, the population of the debtor State would not suffer a loss of purchasing power greater than the amount of their debt.

For all these reasons I have ventured to assert that, at any rate as a matter of economic theory, there is no transfer problem, but only a budgetary problem. And I think that Mr. Keynes will agree with me. But he will observe—and this is his second criticism—that the results mentioned above are true only in economic theory, when it is assumed that all phenomena have free play and are not subject to all the resistances and frictions which in reality paralyze their operation. "In the case of German reparations," he says, "we are trying to fix the volume of foreign remittances and compel the balance of trade to adjust itself thereto. Those who see no difficulty in this . . . are applying the theory of liquids to what is, if not a solid, at least a sticky mass with strong internal resistances."

Thus, Mr. Keynes does not deny the existence of the phenomena that tend to maintain economic equilibria, but he holds that these phenomena are unable to overcome the resistances that in practice oppose the adjustments they tend to bring about. In other words, when the equilibrium of a balance of payments has been disturbed—as it is by the payment of a new debt of a political character—there will, it is true, be a tendency towards the restoration of this equilibrium; but to be effective this tendency will have to modify existing situations and, in particular, bring about profound changes in commercial currents. Mr. Keynes refuses to admit that the stuff of economics is sufficiently fluid to obey rapidly and without profound disturbances the influences of a noneconomic origin that tend to shape it. He considers in particular that the *trade balance* at any moment is largely dependent on the economic structures of the various countries and that it cannot adjust itself rapidly to the requirements of an equilibrium in the balance of payments when the conditions of this equilibrium are abruptly modified.

By means of the foregoing consideration, Mr. Keynes defines the problem with abundant clearness. He thinks that the writers who deny the existence of a transfer problem are wrong in stating that the balance of payments of a country is always brought into equilibrium by the operation of the phenomena of exchange and prices, and that therefore, when the invisible factors of the balance of payments undergo an important change, the trade balance spontaneously undergoes a change in the opposite direction.

If Mr. Keynes is right, there is a transfer problem, and it is necessary to limit continually actual transfers to the transfer possibilities of the moment; if, on the other hand, he is wrong, it is the previous transfers that determine the conditions of equilibrium of the balance of payments, and it would be absurd to attempt to make actual transfers dependent on the transfer possibilities that they themselves create.

To settle the question, it will be sufficient to examine the facts and to inquire whether, in previous cases in which the equilibrium of the balance of payments has been abruptly disturbed, the trade balance has obeyed the phenomena which tend to maintain the equilibrium of the balance of payments, or whether, on the contrary, the adjustment of the trade balance has been rendered impossible by those resistances that Mr. Keynes alleges to exist.

Thus, past experience will tell us in each case the amount of truth contained in Mr. Keynes' assertions, who, as if to help us in examining his contention, has further defined its meaning as follows:

"My own view is that at a given time the economic structure of a country in relation to the economic structure of its neighbors permits of a certain natural level of exports, and that arbitrarily to effect a material alteration of this level by deliberate devices is extremely difficult."

This judgment contains a twofold assertion: first, that for each country there is a "natural" level of exports, determined by the economic structure of the different countries concerned; second, that it is extremely difficult to effect an alteration of this level arbitrarily and deliberately.

I shall first endeavor to refute this second assertion, and will then go on to examine the first. In the course of this discussion I shall have to have resort to arguments I have already used in a previous study,[1] with which I think Mr. Keynes is already acquainted. I have the less scruple in doing so as Mr. Keynes' article shows me that I did not sufficiently bring out the lessons to be derived from this study as regards the sensitiveness of economic phenomena, and particularly as regards the adaptability of balances of payments to certain deliberately provoked situations.

In this work I examined, among other things, the phenomena that followed the most profound and abrupt disturbance ever suffered by a balance of payments—that which was produced by the decision suddenly taken by Great Britain and the United States at the beginning of 1919 to cease granting France the sterling and dollar credits that had previously enabled France's balance of payments to be kept in equilibrium. This decision removed from the credit side of this balance of accounts an item of approximately 20,000 million francs. To use Mr. Keynes' own words, it was "arbitrary" and a "deliberate device."

If our author's contention was correct—in other words, if, as he says, a country's balance of payments is the result of the economic structure of the countries concerned—and if it were extremely difficult to effect a material alteration in the natural level of exports by a deliberate device, France's trade balance should not have been modified. It should have remained, after the removal of the credit, materially what it had been before, since the economic structure of the countries concerned was not affected by the free decision of the British and American Governments. If this had been so, the deficit in France's balance of payments would have been approximately 20,000 million francs per annum.

The facts show, however, that this was by no means the case. In 1919 the deficit in France's trade balance was approximately 23,000 million francs. In 1920, it was approximately the same. But in 1921 it had been reduced to

[1] "An Economic Error: the Organization of Transfers," Chapter IV, above *et seq.*

approximately 2,000 million francs, and remained more or less at that level during 1922 and 1923.

In other words, following upon the cessation of the credits which France received from her Allies, a change had taken place in her trade balance very nearly equal to the amount of the credits withdrawn, this change making up for their disappearance and restoring an equilibrium whose disturbance had nevertheless been deliberate.

It should further be observed that if in 1919 equilibrium was re-established during a period of currency depreciation, this depreciation was not in any way an essential factor of the phenomena that brought about the re-establishment of equilibrium. The latter resulted from a reduction of internal prices as compared with external prices estimated in the national currency, and this diminution, achieved through a rise in the rate of foreign exchange under a fixed price regime, might have been brought about more easily by a diminution, in a very limited amount, in internal prices, in a regime of metallic circulation. The above observation is developed in the work already referred to.

Mr. Keynes will no doubt think that the phenomena referred to above constitute a mere coincidence. The change in the trade balance that seems to make up for the withdrawal of the political credits may, according to him, be only the transition from the "natural level" of the state of war to the "natural level" of the state of peace, and may have simply been caused by the changes in economic structure attending this transformation.

If this were so, it would still be somewhat surprising that the change in the trade balance should coincide approximately with the amount of the credits withdrawn. But, further, the trade balance should remain more or less constant after this movement, or rather it should only undergo changes provoked by modifications in the economic structure of the countries concerned.

The facts, however, were quite otherwise. France's trade balance remained practically constant during 1921, 1922, and 1923 (deficit, in millions of francs, 2,295, 2,552, and 2,256).

But during 1924 it underwent a further striking change, and showed no longer a deficit, but a surplus of 1,540 million francs.

Now everyone knows that the end of the year 1923 witnessed in France the beginning of the great period of the exportation of capital. This introduced a new debit item in the balance of payments. If, therefore, the trade balance had remained unchanged, the balance of payments would have shown a deficit. To bring about equilibrium, a modification of a trade balance was necessary. Now this modification displayed itself at the very moment when theory would have led one to expect it. In fact, a surplus was recorded, although never since 1875 had the Customs statistics revealed in France a surplus of exports over imports.[1]

This surplus was maintained during the year 1925 (1,660 million francs). During 1926 it fell to 80 million, and again rose in 1927 to 1,875 million francs. But from 1928 onward, i.e., from about a year and a half after the end of the great capital export crisis,[2] the deficit reappeared. It amounted to 2,101 million francs, i.e., it returned to about the figure of the years 1921, 1922, and 1923, during which it was generally acknowledged that in France there was no movement for the export of capital.

Thus, during all this period France's trade balance has always adjusted itself very definitely to the modifications in the financial factors of the balance of payments (first political credits and then investments abroad), although these modifications were extremely rapid and involved exceptionally large amounts, and although they had no relation to what Mr. Keynes calls the economic structure of the countries concerned.

That the trade balance adjusted itself to the quite exceptional volume of investments abroad during the great crisis of exportation of capital that occurred in France for psycho-

[1] Except, however, in 1905, when there was an exceptional surplus of 88 million francs.

[2] After the withdrawal of the political credits in 1919, it also took about one and a half years for the trade balance to adjust itself.

logical reasons definitely invalidates the opinion which Mr. Keynes expressed as follows:

"Historically the volume of foreign investment has tended, I think, to adjust itself, at least to a certain extent, to the balance of trade rather than the other way round, the former being the sensitive and the latter the insensitive factor."

We have just shown that in France, after the war, the exact contrary proved to be true.

At all times, in fact, the trade balance has shown a tendency to adjust itself to the necessities of the equilibrium of the balance of payments, whatever they might be and whatever their origin. Between 1870 and 1914, for instance, France's trade balance only showed a surplus during the period 1872–75, during which France was rapidly paying off the war debt imposed on her by Germany; while during all the rest of this period the trade balance showed a deficit of several hundred million francs per annum.

There is the exception, however, of the year 1905, as indicated in note 1 on the preceding page. For the period 1867–87 the figures are as follows:

Year	Trade balance	Year	Trade balance
1867	− 201	1877	− 243
1868	− 514	1878	− 997
1869	− 79	1879	− 1,364
1870	− 65	1880	− 1,566
1871	− 694	1881	− 1,302
1872	+ 191	1882	− 1,247
1873	+ 233	1883	− 1,353
1874	+ 194	1884	− 1,111
1875	+ 336	1885	− 1,000
1876	− 413	1886	− 960

Clearly, there could be no question of a modification of what Mr. Keynes calls the "natural" level of exports, as the needs not satisfied during the war obviously tended to increase the deficit in the trade balance during the period following the close of hostilities. The appearance of a surplus at a time when all the resistances invoked by Mr. Keynes should have made it impossible, although it was a necessary condition of the equilibrium of the balance of payments, provides a fresh example of the extreme elasticity of economic matter and of its powers of adaptation, even when the disturbing phenomenon is "arbitrary" and "artificially produced."

It should be pointed out, however, that during the period France's trade balance sometimes showed a surplus—for instance, from 1862 to 1866. But it is obvious that the payment of a foreign debt can appear in the trade balance only if all conditions are equal with regard to the invisible elements of balance of payments. What is remarkable in the case of France after 1870 is that a surplus appeared in the trade balance at precisely the moment when theory would lead one to expect it. This only constitutes a presumption—but a very strong presumption—in favor of the said theory.

The modifications undergone since the war by the various balances of payments provide, moreover, a still more decisive proof of the extraordinary power of the machinery that tends to maintain the equilibrium of balances or payments or to restore it when it has been artificially disturbed. At the same time they permit us to form an estimate of Mr. Keynes' judgment that "at a given time the economic structure of a country in relation to the economic structure of its neighbors permits of a certain *natural* level of exports."

In 1913, France's trade balance showed a deficit of 1,540 million francs. This deficit was practically the same as that of 1912 (1,518 million francs). The situation that it indicated was the outcome of entirely normal conditions.

After the war, on the contrary, a quarter of the national territory—and the area which furnished France with by far the greatest proportion of her exports—had become unproductive. At the same time, an immense market with almost boundless requirements was created within the country for the reconstruction of the devastated areas.

For all these reasons, the country should have found extreme difficulty in exporting and could have imported to an unlimited extent. The "natural level" of the trade balance, that resulting from the economic structure of the different countries concerned, should have involved a deficit much greater than before the war. If, therefore, Mr. Keynes' views were correct, there should, in fact, have been such a deficit.

It is true that if such a deficit existed it would have produced a deficit in the balance of payments of the country, since clearly the invisible assets of this balance of payments were not greater after the war than before. This, however, is impossible according to the writers who maintain that the balance of payments of a country is always in equilibrium.

Further, if the views of these writers are correct, the deficit shown in 1912 and 1913 by France's trade balance must have been compensated by a surplus of invisible exports, and it was generally acknowledged before the war that the great part of this surplus was formed by the income from foreign investments held by Frenchmen. During the war, however, these holdings greatly diminished. Many of the foreign securities that they comprised were handed over to the State at its request, in exchange for French bonds, and were disposed of by it. Others, particularly Russian securities, became unproductive. If, therefore, the deficit of the trade balance had remained after the war what it was in 1913, France's balance of payments would certainly have shown a deficit also. For this balance to be brought into equilibrium—and the writers whom Mr. Keynes criticizes consider that, whatever the resistances of the economic milieu, a balance of payments is bound to be in equilibrium[1]—it was essential that after the war, in spite of all adverse circumstances, the deficit in the French trade balance should be lower than what it was in 1913.

Here, therefore, we have a crucial test of the two theories, that of Mr. Keynes and that of the writers who deny the existence of a transfer problem. If France's trade balance since the war shows a greater deficit than in 1913, the theory of the "natural" level must be true. Otherwise it is the theory which Mr. Keynes criticizes that must be accepted.

[1] Except during a period of budget deficits or flight from the currency. It is clear that when the holders of foreign currency do not repatriate the equivalent, equilibrium can never be attained.

The deficit of 1,540 million francs for 1913 was equivalent to about 297 million francs.

In 1921, on the other hand, imports exceeded exports by 2,295 million French francs. The average rate of the dollar in francs during the same year was 13.49. Hence the deficit in the trade balance represented approximately 170 million dollars, or 57 per cent of the 1913 figure.

In 1922, the deficit in France's trade balance was 2,552 million French francs, and the average rate of the dollar was frs. 12.33. The deficit in the trade balance was therefore 206 million dollars, or 69 per cent of the 1913 figure.

This result would be still more striking if we took into account the level of prices rather than the rates of exchange in comparing the deficits before and after the war.

Thus, despite the most unfavorable circumstances imaginable, the deficit in France's balance of trade was very materially lower in 1921 and 1922 than it was in 1913, although during the former period the reduction in the country's export capacity, owing to the entire destruction of its most active factories on the one hand and its enoromus reconstruction needs on the other, would have led one to expect a considerable increase in the deficit in its trade balance. This unexpected result seems to decide between the two theories by showing that the most powerful "natural" resistances cannot prevent the restoration of the equilibrium of the balance of payments, even when the equilibrium has been disturbed by events of a purely financial nature. It shows, moreover, that the notion of a "natural" level of exports is a complete fallacy and cannot legitimately be invoked.

This conclusion would be brought out still more clearly if we could analyze here the machinery by which the equilibrium of the balance of payments is maintained in current practice. We have attempted this analysis elsewhere.[1] Suffice it to say that it led to the conclusion that, apart from periods

[1] *Théorie des phénomènes monétaires* (Payot, Paris), 2nd Part—and particularly Chapter VIII, Sections 2, 3, and 4. A summary of the theory was given in the foregoing study: "An Economic error: the Organization of Transfers, Chapter IV, *et seq.* See in particular also the second part of this work.

of "flight from the currency" and of budget deficits, exchange and price movements tending to maintain the equilibrium of the balance of payments are bound to go on until the previous equilibrium has been completely re-established.

The same theory provides an answer to Mr. Keynes' objection that the raising of foreign Customs tariffs might make it impossible to restore the equilibrium of a balance of payments by making the increase in exports required for this restoration impossible. It is quite clear, of course, that if there is a mechanism tending to restore the equilibrium of balances of payments when it has been accidentally disturbed, this mechanism must prevent the raising of the Customs barriers which surround a country from modifying the result of that country's balance of payments.[2] This is indeed evident *a priori*, for if a change in Customs duties affected balances of payments, it would be possible, by raising simultaneously *all* Customs tariffs, to make *all* balances of payments show a surplus, which is absurd. As this is impossible, there must be a mechanism that prevents changes in Customs tariffs from disturbing the equilibrium in balances of payments, and this mechanism is bound to be effective at whatever level Customs duties are fixed. In the work mentioned above,[1] we have shown that experience very clearly confirmed the accuracy of these theoretical views when the United States put a new Customs tariff into force in 1922.

Thus, in the different examples we have considered, the equilibrium of the balance of payments has always been restored, whatever the extent of the initial disturbance and however arbitrary it may have been.

We do not say, however, that unlimited sums could be transferred from one country to another; we simply observe

[2] We are speaking here only of the balance of payments, i.e., the difference between the value of credit and debit items. It is clear, of course, that a modification in the Customs tariff, by modifying the relative prices of the various foreign goods, modifies the exchanges of these goods and therefore modifies the constitution and value of imports and exports.

[1] *Les répercussions monétaires d'une politique douanière: l'application du tarif Fordney aux Etats-Unis en 1922*. Théorie des phénomènes monétaires, p. 305.

that in the cases we have just studied the disturbance in the equilibrium of the balance of payments was greater than that which would result from the normal application of the Dawes Plan or the Young Plan, and that equilibrium was always spontaneously restored without interference of any kind.

A complete theory of the phenomenon would show, however, that only sums taken from the resources of a balanced budget could be transferred. It would also indicate, as was said before, that monetary depreciation is by means essential to the operation of the phenomena that restore the balance of payments to equilibrium.

We do not, however, desire to go into such considerations here. The chief aim of the present study was to gauge the truth contained in Mr. Keynes' assertion that to deny the existence of a transfer problem was to apply the theory of liquids to what in reality was, if not a solid, at least a sticky mass.

In every case, however, we have seen economic matter adjust itself with extraordinary elasticity to the influences to which it was subject, whatever their origin, and always, too, we have seen the phenomenon that theory taught us to expect govern the facts that responded in the most sensitive manner. Fluidity of the economic mass, sensitiveness of the phenomena that occur therein, we regard these as two essential observations of infinitely greater consequence than the transfer problem.

To believe, indeed, that resistances due to the very nature of things can prevent economic equilibria from spontaneously establishing or maintaining themselves, is to force oneself to admit the necessity of establishing them by concerted and systematic measures similar to those that would have to be taken by the Transfer Committee to ensure the equilibrium of Germany's balance of payments on the lines of the Dawes Plan. Such a conception leads inevitably to the practice of an *organized economy* similar in principle, if not in object, to the Communist economy.

To admit, on the other hand, that economic phenomena, left to themselves, are able in actual fact to restore or maintain with great exactness the necessary equilibria, leads to the view that the only effective means of avoiding or attenuating economic crisis is to remove or attenuate any obstacles that may stand in the way of spontaneous adjustment, and to avoid all measures that tend to immobilize the various factors of economic equilibrium.

Thus, to gauge the actual sensitiveness of economic phenomena, is to seek the solution of perhaps the most important political problem at present awaiting issue, that of the choice between the two tendencies of liberal economy and organized economy. It is on this ground that the question raised by Mr. Keynes—that of the mobility of economic equilibria—has seemed to us fundamental from the political point of view still more than from the point of view of economic theory. We have endeavored to answer it in the limited sphere of international exchanges; we believe that it is worth systematic study in all spheres of economic life. Perhaps we shall endeavor in a future article to show that the conclusion we have reached is an extremely general one, and that in almost every case a systematic observation of the facts reveals the existence of economic phenomena attaining an unsuspected degree of sensitiveness and permanence.

5

AN ALL-TIME FALLACY:

THE TRADE BALANCE

ARGUMENT

Over the past ten years, most of the measures that have had the effect of isolating the national economies from one another were justified by totally erroneous arguments in the minds of those who, in all good faith, thought it their duty to advocate them. I cannot possibly attempt to consider within the framework of this address all the spurious reasonings that abound in the economic field. I would like, however, to bring out the most important among them: the one that claims to justify both tariff increases on the one hand and import quotas and exchange controls on the other, by the need for governments to safeguard the equilibrium of their trade balances.

When one peruses speeches made in France, Britain, or other countries by responsible statesmen, one nearly always finds that they express their fears over the aggravation of the trade deficit and their desire to improve the balance of international trade.

The present study is an extract from a lecture given at the new "Ecole de la Paix" on February 27, 1933, entitled: "De quelques hérésies économiques qui ravagent le monde." ("A Few Economic Heresies that Plague the World.") The original text was published in the *Revue d'Economie politique* (Librairie du Recueil Sirey), No. 2, 1933.

Indeed, the course that statesmen ought to take in this field is already mapped out by the universally accepted terminology; from time immemorial, it has indeed been acknowledged that the trade balance of a country is "favorable" when the value of exports is in excess of the value of imports, and that it bespeaks a deficit—in other words, is "unfavorable"—if the reverse obtains.

Now, there is no worthy citizen who does not wish his country to be in the most favorable position possible and who, for this reason, does not wish to see its trade balance improved.

In point of fact, such collective preoccupations are expressed vigorously by all Chambers of Commerce and all the associations which have taken it upon themselves to inspire, keep check of, and sometimes correct the line of policy followed by the public authorities. There is hardly any resolution by a Chamber of Commerce or by a trade or industrial group that does not note with alarm that the trade balance shows a deficit and that such deficit is increasing at a disquieting rate.

It must be conceded, in this field at least, that the governments have vouchsafed on those whom they govern the benefits of their utmost solicitude.

For the past ten years—and above all since the Great Depression—there has not been one Prime Minister, not one Trade Minister, who has not proclaimed on all occasions his firm resolve to devote all his efforts to the improvement of the trade balance of his country.

And those have not been empty promises. For the past ten years, the public authorities have done their utmost to increase exports and to reduce imports. To that end, governments have time and time again resorted to tariff increases, further aggravated by the introduction of import quotas and in certain countries by exchange controls.

Thus, all the governments in the world are bent on improving their national trade balances.

And yet if we consider the situation of just a few European countries, we see that in 1930 Britain, France, the Netherlands, Belgium, and Switzerland had an unfavorable trade balance, and that in the same year Germany, Poland, Rumania, Hungary, and Bulgaria had a favorable trade balance.

You will, I hope, allow me to entertain at least some shreds of doubt as to the meaning of words or the common sense of men when I note that to improve a country's situation consists in bringing it from the situation of France or Britain in 1930 to the situation of Poland, Hungary, or Bulgaria in the same year.

Furthermore, what is true space-wise is no less so in terms of time. Between 1870 and 1933, the French trade balance always showed a deficit except during four years—1872, 1873, 1874, and 1875 and also in 1924, 1925, and 1927.[1]

There again, am I not entitled to entertain some doubts when confronted with a terminology under which the situation wherein France found itself in the darkest hours of its history is dubbed a "favorable" situation, when after the 1870 war it had to make great sacrifices in order to pay a foreign country a very high war indemnity, or when around the years 1924–26 France was in the throes of a confidence crisis and suffered from a capital drain that tended to wreck its currency?

These terminological doubts were strongly confirmed when I read a tale by Bastiat that I should like to relate to you here.

Once upon a time, the story goes—because it begins like a fairy tale and it is indeed a fairy tale since you find in it the magic secret which enables you to turn the trade balance of all countries into a surplus, and thereby to fulfil the wishes of all the heads of government, all the ministers, and all the Chambers of Commerce in the world—there was a master mariner who carried cargo between France and Britain. In those days, the skippers bought their cargo themselves and sold it abroad. This one was a good tradesman and a good mariner. This one bought claret that he had carefully selected

[1] In 1904 and 1905, however, exports nearly equated imports, but had a very slight edge. In all other years except those mentioned in the text, the deficit was substantial.

and paid one million francs for. Then he sailed for England, and when he left port, the watchful Customs officers recorded exports valued at one million francs.

After an uneventful voyage, the ship reached the banks of the Thames and laid anchor there, whereupon the skipper sold his cargo to fine connoisseurs who paid the equivalent in sterling of two million francs.

But our good skipper, as ever a good tradesman, used the two million francs that he had just received to buy cotton goods that were so carefully selected and so cheaply purchased that upon the ship's arrival in France the Customs officers estimated the value of the cargo at four million francs.

Thus our clever tradesman had introduced into the French trade balance an export item of one million francs and an import item of four million francs, representing a deficit of three million francs. His reprehensible activity had therefore aggravated by three million francs France's un-favorable trade balance, and you will agree with me that if words mean anything and if those who want to improve the trade balance of their countries are sensible persons, our skipper should have swung for it, or at least have been re-duced to harmlessness by losing his ticket.

Fortunately, however, Bastiat was not acquainted only with such evildoers. There were among his acquaintances two other mariners: one was a bad tradesman, the other a very poor sailor.

The bad tradesman, for his part, had a capital of four million francs when about to leave Bordeaux, and he bought wine to that amount with the intention of exporting it to Britain. Meticulous as ever, the Customs officers entered an export item amounting to four million francs.

Unfortunately, our exporter had chosen his wine poorly and tended it very badly during the voyage. The British pur-chasers were of opinion that this was the foulest of sour wines and would not pay more than two million francs for it. But the skipper was nevertheless persevering. With the two million francs he too bought cotton goods, but as he was in-competent in this field as well, his was a bad purchase and upon arriving in France the cargo was valued by the Customs officers at its real price in the French market, i.e., one million francs.

Our good skipper had of course ruined himself on his voyage, since he had lost three million francs out of his original capital; yet he had introduced into the French trade balance an export item of four million francs and an import item of one million, leaving an export surplus of three million francs. Everyone ought to have held him in high esteem, and I only hope that all the honors which the then Trade Minister must have vouchsafed him could offset in his heart and mind the bitterness of his ruin.

As to the third skipper—the bad sailor—he sailed from Bordeaux with three million francs worth of wines, excellently selected, out of which he expected to make a substantial profit in the London market. The ever-watchful Customs officers entered an export item of three million francs. Unfortunately, upon sailing out of the harbor, our clumsy skipper ran his ship onto a reef and the ship foundered. The cargo was lost, and all the crew were drowned except the skipper, who was rescued and was thus in a position to know that his clumsiness had introduced into the French trade balance an export item of three million francs that was fully unrequited, and had therefore improved the French trade balance by three million francs.

Thus, the magic formula for redressing a country's trade balance is to buy at high prices at home and to sell at low prices abroad—i.e., to ruin oneself—or to send all the products of domestic industry to the bottom of the sea. You will surely concede that this observation might well shake the conviction of those who believe that it is the duty of governments to reduce the trade deficit or to increase the trade surplus of the country.

One has therefore some reason to question the very meaning of the words and to try in all liberty to determine what to think of a theory which requires that the Customs policy of a country should be aimed at safeguarding or improving the national trade balance.

To make the contention under review more specific still, let us consider its most characteristic expression: the latest report by the National Economic Council on "international trade and the French Customs policy during the Great Depression."

I wish, in the first place, to pay a tribute to the clarity and moderation of this document. I also wish to congratulate its author, M. Adéodat Boissard, on the conscientious manner in which he carried out the task entrusted to him. The adoption of his recommendations by the National Economic Council was a major attempt in the direction of wisdom; the Council realized that a trade deficit is generally offset by invisible resources such as insurance, banking, or transport earnings. But it is very concerned about variations in our trade balance because it fears that they might cause a deficit in the French balance of payments. The Council writes as follows:

> In normal times, France can tolerate a certain apparent deficit in its external trade, it being offset by income from tourism and from investments abroad. But the shortfalls experienced in 1931 and those which seem to be heralded by the provisional results of the first six months of this financial year are of such magnitude that they obviously exceed invisible exports which, too, are declining substantially. The general balance of payments of France is very probably in deficit even now. This is a situation *which must be prevented at all costs from deteriorating further.*
>
> To that end, the following main remedies must be resorted to:
> 1. An attempt to bring down the cost of living in France;
> 2. The revision of some of our trade agreements, in particular the most important one which is the Franco-German agreement.

The contention as expounded above was stated with great clarity and in complete good faith. Allow me, however, to affirm that notwithstanding my great respect for the National Economic Council, I cannot in any way concur with its conclusion. Let us begin first with a detail. The National Economic Council is of opinion that the general balance of accounts in France is "very probably in deficit even now" and reaches this conclusion whereas during the period under consideration—the year 1931 and the first six months of 1932 —the gold reserves of the Bank of France had increased by no less than 28,500 million francs.

I know that there will be many comments about this observation and that people will say that the gold inflow into France results from movements on capital account and that the intention was only to take into consideration the normal items in the balance of payments. But if, leaving aside movements on capital account, the French balance of payments showed a deficit, such deficit would have offset the capital movements and there would be no gold movements. If gold is being imported, the reason is that there is no deficit. This, then, is the first criticism: It is on the basis of a questionable conclusion that a certain policy is recommended, and there can be no doubt that it will furthermore have dire consequences.

But there is more. The figures cited above show that the trade balances of all the wealthy countries show a deficit, notwithstanding the efforts of such countries to maximize exports and minimize imports, whereas the trade balances of the poor countries show a surplus.

Does it follow that the balances of payments of the former show a deficit and that the balances of payments of the latter show a surplus? Assuredly not. The wealthy countries have foreign currency resources that do not appear in their trade balances, in particular income from foreign securities held by their nationals. If their balances of payments are to be equilibrated, their trade balances must be in deficit and this is what happens in practice. On the other hand, poor countries have received loans from abroad. They have to service those loans every year. If their balances of payments are to be equilibrated, their trade balances must show a surplus, and here again, experience shows that this is exactly what happens.

Admittedly, the United States seems to be an exception to this rule. But this is only a deceptive appearance. The United

States, which has been a rich country since the war, had a trade surplus because every year it used to reinvest abroad all the resources accruing to it abroad. But since the Great Depression set in, it has stopped granting loans abroad—hence, the fact that its trade surplus declined from 744 million dollars in 1929 to 288 million dollars in 1931.

Indeed, this is an absolute rule and I know of no exceptions to it. Whenever a new debit element has appeared in the balance-of-payments of a country, the trade balance has worked the necessary adjustments, and equilibrium has been promptly restored.

France, which is a rich country, has always had a trade deficit except during the 1924–25 period when confidence was lacking. During that period, exports of capital introduced a substantial debit item into the French balance of payments. The trade balance forthwith worked the necessary adjustment and its traditional deficit was turned into an appreciable surplus. But in 1927, exports of capital ceased and no later than the following year the deficit was again at about its previous level, i.e., roughly 2,000 million francs.

From then on, a dual phenomenon emerged: We began regularly to receive appreciable amounts in the form of German reparations, while the astounding French monetary recovery attracted to that country idle capital from abroad. For these two reasons there was a demand for francs in the market, i.e., a new and increasing credit element in the French balance of payments. If the trade balance had remained at its previous level, the balance of accounts would have been in surplus. But that was not the case, because the trade deficit began increasing immediately, rising from 2,000 million francs in 1928 to 8,100 million in 1929, 9,900 million in 1930, and 11,800 million in 1931.

In 1931, we ceased receiving German reparations payments and the inflow of capital into France slowed down. The deficit immediately fell, from 11,800 million in 1931 to 10,100 million in 1932.

You can appreciate how futile were the fears of the National Economic Council which wrote in its report:

Now that reparations payments have ended, the need to balance our trade must have precedence.

Have no fear, expert gentlemen, equilibrium is well secured and was so even before you took it upon yourselves to put the matter in the forefront of your preoccupations.

Moreover, it has been possible to observe similar phenomena in all similar cases. The example of Germany is peremptory in this respect.

Between 1924 and 1930, Germany nearly always borrowed large sums from abroad except in 1926 and in 1930, as the report of the Basle experts notes.

Now, in those two years, the German trade balance that usually showed a deficit—as is always the case when a country borrows money from abroad—showed a surplus of 800 million marks in 1926 and 1,500 million marks in 1930.

But there is more. Commencing in March 1931, not only did Germany cease borrowing money from abroad, but it was also affected by a very intensive capital export movement that introduced into its balance of payments a new and very substantial debit element. As everything led one to expect, Germany's trade surplus increased forthwith, to the point where in 1931 it reached the extraordinary figure of 3,000 million marks—equivalent to 18,000 million francs. This surplus was all the more remarkable as it occurred during a period of world-wide depression and despite sales difficulties and restrictions of all kinds.

The result is the same in each and every case. This can be observed from the trade balance of all the Balkan countries, as it had been possible to observe after 1870 in the French trade balance.

Always, at any time, whenever a new element is introduced into the balance of payments of a country, the trade balance moves in such a way that the balance of international commitments is maintained.

And where no abrupt disturbance occurs, then imports and exports move in the same direction, in the same proportion, so that balance-of-payments equilibrium can be maintained.

This conclusion is in the form of a rule that suffers no exceptions. Apart from cases of flight from the currency or where there is a budget deficit—and those, one must admit, are fundamental exceptions—the balance of payments of a country is always in equilibrium. And as such equilibrium cannot be doubted, the question is whether this general phenomenon can be regarded as fortuitous or whether, on the contrary, it is the product of a mechanism which is of a permanent nature.

To answer the question, one need only analyze the formation of trade balances. In the case of France, for instance, any person who, anywhere in the world, drinks a glass of claret or champagne introduces a debit item into our trade balance, and any person who, anywhere in France, eats chocolate or wears English cloth introduces a debit item. Now, all such persons act in all places throughout the world in a completely unrelated manner, without ever being concerned about the effects of their acts on the general situation of the country. In addition, no authority in any part of the world—except in Soviet Russia—attempts to co-ordinate their actions and to adjust purchases abroad to foreign sales.

And yet it is an unquestionable fact that a marvelous equilibrium obtains at each moment between the credit and debit sides of the ledger, and this is achieved with sufficient accuracy for a new offsetting credit item to appear forthwith whenever a new debit item emerges.

Thus, the conclusion cannot be evaded. This equilibrium that no one establishes and that cannot be coincidental is the result of an all-powerful mechanism that succeeds in a continuing manner in adjusting debts to claims and in ensuring the equilibrium of external commitments without which no country could endure.

Bear it in mind that all courses in political economy teach that balances of payments are assured and maintained in constant equilibrium as a result of exchange and price phenomena. But though everyone is familiar with this teaching, no one believes in it. I would very much like to have convinced you that it is a disastrous mistake to forget that in fact, at each moment, everywhere and always, balance-of-payments equilibrium is assured by a mechanism that never fails so long as there is no flight from the national currency nor any budget deficit.

To tell the truth, I am not convinced that in the classical theory the description of the phenomenon is quite accurate. I believe that the explanation is rather more subtle than the one generally advanced; but what cannot be denied is that the phenomenon is real and that it governs the facts in a very strict way. The trade balance has always been, in all circumstances, what it had to be for the balance of payments to be in equilibrium, i.e., for the country to endure, and with a precision that no State intervention could ever claim to achieve.

Accordingly, you can appreciate how preposterous it is for governments to claim that they can bring the trade balance to the right level so that balance-of-payments equilibrium should not be jeopardized, how preposterous it is on the part of all our statesmen to vow that their people can rest assured because they are keeping watch and will take all necessary steps to adjust commercial exchanges to current needs, and lastly how unjustified the Economic Council was when it made its learned recommendation as follows:

> "The general balance of payments of France is very probably in deficit even now. This is a situation which must be prevented at all costs from deteriorating further."

Do these governments seriously believe that it was a result of their solicitude that the French trade balance showed a surplus in 1870? Do they believe that it was as a result of their solicitude that in 1931 the French trade balance showed the deficit that we have noted—a deficit which was essential if balance-of-payments equilibrium was to be safeguarded, just as the tremendous German trade surplus was essential—a trade surplus that soared so high that no government could ever have hoped to achieve it.

Thus, our governments stand in relation to our trade balance in the same position as Rostand's Chanticleer in relation to the sun that he thought would not rise unless he crowed. Every day, to make it rise, he crowed to sing its praises, just as every day someone in the world, some Trade Minister, solemnly proclaims that he is going to take the necessary steps to ward off possible disturbances in the trade balance.

One could still be indulgent if this was a mere error of no consequence. Chanticleer, after all, inconvenienced no one but himself by singing the sun's praises. But if, in order to pursue this daydreaming, he had starved his farmyard friends, then he would have been guilty and it would have been incumbent upon the just to disillusion him.

Now, the trade balance fallacy is certainly not something that is of no consequence for economic life. A host of measures have been introduced on its behalf. I do not contend that they have been inspired solely by the desire to safeguard the trade balance. I am saying that the argument used in justification was the need to avoid any aggravation of the deficit, and it was this argument that on many occasions convinced those who were carrying out the steps or those who were advocating them.

All the foregoing has shown you, I hope, that this argument was in contradiction to all known facts.

We cannot but recognize that everything that has been determined on the basis of this argument is groundless and therefore unwarranted.

Unwarranted is the word as regards tariff increases instituted to ward off an aggravation of the trade deficit—unwarranted and unavailing, because the trade balance is just as insensitive to them as the movements of the sun were to the crowing of Chanticleer. And surely this was bound to be so, for if governments could influence the trade balance of their country by resorting to Customs duties, it would be within their power to generate trade surpluses for every country at the same time, which would be a contradiction in terms and therefore a preposterous proposition.

Furthermore, should not the example of France have taught us that Customs duties did not make it possible to counteract an increase in the trade deficit, since in 1931 when the disruption mentioned above occurred, the protective wall with which we surrounded ourselves did not succeed in forestalling the inflow of foreign goods into France.

It is true that our governments did not acknowledge defeat. They resorted to another method, a method which cannot fail when one is trying to stem the flow of imports: I refer to the quota system. But there again, experience has shown that however efficient this device may be for reducing imports, it did not succeed in altering the trade balance appreciably because it affected to a roughly similar extent the quantum of exports.

And the same holds true with exchange controls, which enable the central authority to prohibit all imports. All such methods, however efficient they may be for minimizing foreign trade, have only a very limited influence on the trade balance that is always what it has to be in order that the balance of payments may be in equilibrium, account being taken of all the acts, desires, and mistakes of individuals. In this field, the duty of governments is to remain blind to trade statistics, never to worry about them, and never to take any steps with a view to altering them.

And notwithstanding all the liking for statistics that is attributed to me, I would not hesitate to recommend the elimination of foreign trade statistics if the question were put to me, in view of all the harm that they have done in the past, that they are still doing and, I am very much afraid, will continue to do in the future.

But, you may ask, if you cease struggling against an increase in the trade deficit, do you resign yourself to such a deficit when it occurs? On this point again, I have no hesitation in replying that when a trade deficit occurs that is not the result of a budget deficit, there is no other solution but to accept it, because when the deficit occurs, the reason is that it is essential in order that balance-of-payments equilibrium may be safeguarded.

Whenever in the past a trade deficit has increased, the reason was that a new source of foreign claims had emerged:

reparations, inflow of capital looking for safety, or income from foreign securities.

We are thus left with the view that, notwithstanding the commonly accepted opinion, a trade deficit—which is the essential feature of the situation of all the countries that are both long-established and rich—is a sign of wealth, whereas an excess of exports over imports is nearly always the hallmark of real poverty.

ELEMENTS FOR A

BALANCE-OF-

PAYMENTS

THEORY

ELEMENTS FOR A

BALANCE-OF-PAYMENTS

THEORY

The facts of equilibrium and disequilibrium expounded in Part One of this book do exist. They are too numerous, too precise, and too improbable to be regarded as fortuitous.

The reserve that the great majority of economists show in their regard is evidence that to those economists they do not seem to bear the mark of verisimilitude and that, in any case, classical theory—i.e., the theory of "comparative advantages" —offers no explanation for them.

They are the basis of a real theory of international trade that I have relentlessly vindicated ever since I became aware of the concomitant phenomena that make quite unquestionable the existence and efficiency of a mechanism tending to ensure equilibrium in international trade, in the absence, that is, of inflation and the gold-exchange standard.

In my first attempts at an explanation, my thinking was still characterized by too many vestiges of quantitativism.

However, as early as 1927 in my "Théorie des Phénomènes monétaires"[1] ("Theory of Monetary Phenomena") I contended that the surplus of "total demand" in relation to "total supply"—today one says "aggregate supply and aggregate demand"—was the prime mover of variations in the

[1] Payot, Paris (out of print).

general level of prices and, as a result, of balances of payments. I was, however, underestimating the direct and immediate action of variations in aggregate demand on outlets, which today would be called the "income effect."

It was in 1928, on the occasion of the debate between John Maynard Keynes and me, which I have mentioned above, that I expounded for the first time the dominant role of variations in aggregate demand on balances of payments.

Although it was many years ago, I remember it vividly. Lord Keynes and I were standing before a large audience, on the platform of a concert hall in Geneva.

While I was stating the reasons why the balance of payments of a country was always in equilibrium if there were no characterized inflationary phenomena there, Keynes, who was pacing up and down, cut me short and said: "But how do you expect such equilibrium to come about?"

I retorted: "Because if part of the national income is spent abroad, it will not be available for the purchase, at the market price, of part of domestic production representing the same value. That part will remain available for export. If those products which cannot be sold domestically find a foreign purchaser immediately, balance-of-payments equilibrium will be restored. If not, prices will tend to fall in the deficit country until they reach the level where an equivalent part of the national product is exported."

"Well, well," said Keynes, resuming his pacing. "This is an interesting idea. I must give it some thought."

I too have given it further thought in attempting to find out whether there were precise relations between aggregate demand and aggregate supply.

Naturally, the law of outlets—the law of Jean-Baptiste Say —said that there were. But in saying so, it denied any possibility of inflation and any possibility of action by the credit policy on international trade and on prices.

It was obvious that the law of outlets overlooked the monetary influences that can cause aggregate demand to differ from the aggregate value of supplies.

It was in "L'Ordre social" ("Social Order"), the first edition of which dates back to 1924, that I formulated the basic theorem of aggregate demand:

> The difference between aggregate demand and aggregate supply is at any time strictly equal to the difference between the aggregate variations in the amount of effective cash balances and in that of the desired cash balances.[1]

This formulation shows that the law of outlets is true only to the extent that the quantity of money in circulation remains permanently at the same level as the aggregate amount of desired cash balances.

It brings out the dual nature of market phenomena that include a purchasing power component—the income-effect—and a monetary component—the currency-effect. Above all, it demonstrates that the two aspects are indissolubly linked by some kind of fundamental complementarity, reminiscent of the complementarity link between the wave and the corpuscle in undulatory mechanics.

Yet the above-mentioned theorem did not bring out any link between the issue of money and a variation in the aggregate amount of desired cash balances. It was obvious, however, that such a relation did exist. Indeed, it had never happened that the holder of a cash balance who wished to increase the amount thereof, for instance on the eve of a holiday or with a view to paying the bills falling due at the end of the month, was prevented from doing so.

The aggregate behavior of the money users therefore had an influence on the monetary issue. A comprehensive theory had, of course, to search for the circuitous ways through which individual behavior influenced the creation of money.

This research led me to the certainty that the amount of effective cash balances was closely related to the aggregate amount of desired cash balances and that, as a result, aggregate demand too was related to aggregate supply—the relation not being one of strict equality as Jean-Baptiste Say contended—but by a precise and subtle relation, itself depending on the nature of the assets which are the counterpart of money.

[1] Librairie Médicis, 3rd ed., 1967, p. 282.

The relation between actual cash balances and desired cash balances is a complex one, for it brings into play the delicate and practically unexplored mechanism of forward markets. It is therefore a subtle relation and one which, for that reason, is likely to account for the subtle relations that are reflected in balance-of-payments phenomena.

The result of my first round of research was expounded in 1953 in a short publication entitled "Influences regulating the amount of currency and the institutional problem of money."

Although this study goes far beyond the balance-of-payments question, I have reproduced it in Chapter 6 hereafter because the phenomenon that it brings into relief—the relation between actual cash balances and desired cash balances—is the only one which can account for the relation between aggregate demand and aggregate supply that generates balance-of-payments phenomena. Section 6 of this study deals specifically with "balance-of-payments equilibrium."

After this study was published, however, several friends, in particular the late-lamented Professor Goetz-Girey, told me that my analysis was a complex one and that they had had serious difficulty in following its development.

On their advice, I attempted to submit a less rigorous and simpler statement entitled "Elements for a Theory of the Discount Rate and the Balance of Payments." The text is reproduced in Chapter 7 of this publication.

I would now, if I may, advise the reader who has no particular liking for strict economic theory to skip Chapter 6 and pass on directly to Chapter 7.

6

INFLUENCES
REGULATING THE
AMOUNT OF
CURRENCY AND THE
INSTITUTIONAL
PROBLEM OF
MONEY

On several monetary questions, I find a major difficulty in following the views of some very close friends of mine, whose ideas on other economic problems I fully share.

These difficulties arise essentially from our different views with respect to the influences that determine the volume of money in circulation.

The contrast is not a theoretical one only. Its importance was made quite clear during the discussions of a recent committee of the OEEC on "internal stability." The majority of my colleagues saw in a loan whose proceeds remain unspent a mechanical cause of deflation. They unreservedly espoused the theory so admirably expressed by Keynes in the parable of the dinner: "An act of individual saving means—so to say—a decision not to have dinner to-day. . . . Thus it depresses the business of preparing today's dinner without stimulating the business of making ready for some acts of future consumption."[1] My own ideas, on the contrary, lead me to see in unspent savings an influence that tends to decrease the quantity of money in circulation.

The choice between the two theses entails important consequences both in the field of monetary theory and in that of concrete action. It helps, particularly, to delimit the tasks and the responsibilities that rest on Governments and on Banks of Issue in the fields of investments and currency.

For these various reasons, I have set forth in the following pages the essential elements of my position, so as to submit them for the consideration of those who hold different opinions on the same problems.

The measure of total demand

For the purpose of analyzing the influences that determine the volume of money in circulation, some fundamental notions should be recalled or more precisely defined.

The general level of prices, in each market period, depends only on the ratio between total demand and the total value of supplies.[2]

When prices are free, no distinction need be drawn between the demand and the amount of purchases made.

But the purchases made may be settled in cash or on credit.

When cash payments are made, the money required for

---

1 *General Theory of Employment, Interest and Money,* p. 210.

2 I have shown in my *Théorie des phénomènes monétaires* (Payot, 1927, p. 72) and in my *L'Ordre Social* (3rd ed., Librairie Médicis, 1967, pp. 32–39) that the arithmetical average of all market prices, weighted by the quantities exchanged, is not affected by the distribution of total demand and depends only—all conditions as regards supply remaining the same—on the amount of total demand. This proposition has led me, since 1927, to use "total demand" as the essential instrument in the dynamic analysis of markets.

the payment can come only from a sale made by the purchaser during the same market period; from an excess of the creation, as compared with the destruction, of money effected for his account during the same period; or from a reduction, during the period elapsing between the opening and the closing of the market, of the cash balance he wishes to hold.

This permits us to write:

"The demand of an exchanger during a market period = the amount of proceeds from the sales he has made during that period, + the excess of the creation over the destruction of money effected for his account during that same period, — variations that have occurred, between the opening and the close of the market, in the cash balance he wishes to hold."

If we add, one by one, the analogous equations applicable to all participants in the market, we conclude that in each market period *the total demand is equal to the total value of the supplies, augmented by the difference between the variations, during the same period, in the quantity of money in circulation and the total amount of cash balances desired.*

This identity shows that the bulk of the demand, in each period, is provided by the value of the supplies. Jean Baptiste Say's famous Law of Markets is an approximate, and therefore inaccurate, expression of this proposition. In reality, total demand will deviate from the total value of supplies—and the general level of prices will vary—whenever there is a divergence between the variations, during the period under consideration, in the volume of the currency in circulation and the total amount of cash balances desired.

The identity presented above is therefore a corrected version of the quantity theory of money.

However, for its proper interpretation, an elaboration of the notion of the "cash balance desired" is indispensable.

The "desired" cash balance is made up of all cash that its holder does not wish to replace by wealth of a nonmonetary nature.

Now, the quantity of money in circulation whose existence does not lead to any demand for nonmonetary wealth can be divided into two fractions: that which is required for making settlements relating to transactions effected in the market, and that which individuals wish to keep to meet possible contingencies.

The existence of cash balances that are indispensable for the settlement of previous transactions is the consequence of the fact that most settlement procedures—except for hand-to-hand payments of actual cash—entail delays of appreciable length, during which the sums in question no longer figure among the assets of the payer, and nevertheless do not yet form part of the assets of the payee. This is the case, particularly, when remittances are made by post, or payments are made by check or transfers. Money thus employed represents what accountants call sums "in transit." Its amount determines, at each moment, the volume of money that would have been indispensable for the settlement of transactions already effected, if no sums of money were ever kept in reserve in view of possible needs. For this reason, it represents for us the amount of "necessary cash balances."

The total volume of necessary cash balances will obviously depend on the settlement procedures actually used, on the volume of transactions to be settled, and on the general price level. If the community considered "revolves" in a regular way, the first of these factors will not change. Then the amount of the necessary cash balances will depend only on the movement of trade and on the price level. In all cases, the total amount of the necessary cash balances is mechanically determined by economic and financial factors.

With respect to the volume of "cash balances hoarded" for possible use, it depends to a large extent on the expectations entertained by the users of money as to the amount of their future needs. It is determined essentially by psychological factors.

An important difference exists between hoarded and necessary cash balances. The former are found in cashboxes or in purses. Hence, their existence and their amount are known to their holders, whereas the latter, being "in transit," are not apparent, except to accountants.

"Necessary and hoarded cash balances," taken together, determine the amount of cash balances which their holders do not wish to replace by goods of a nonmonetary nature. For this reason, we describe them as "desired cash balances."[1]

The identity established above, which relates the difference between total demand and total supply to the difference between variations in the volume of currency in circulation and the total amount of desired cash balances, recalls the classical quantity theory.

It differs from it, however, in substituting the notion of desired cash balances for that of the velocity of circulation of money. The following paragraphs will show that the former, though of a psychological nature, has a quality of economic reality that is entirely lacking in the purely arithmetical expression represented by the latter.

Like the classical theory, our "quantity identity" does not permit us to localize the cause of inflationary phenomena either in the first or in the second member of the equation. All that it teaches us is that if one of them varies, the other will vary in the same proportion.

Nevertheless, if we wish to avoid, in the case of this renewed form of the quantity theory, the error so often committed in the case of the old one, if we wish to prevent its being only a formal relation void of economic content, then we must penetrate into the mechanism by which the identity of the two members of the equation is, in fact, assured. This is what will be attempted in the following paragraphs.

Credit and discounting

The preceding analysis is based on the hypothesis of immediate settlements. I am now going to inquire into the consequences of deferring payment, i.e., of credit.

To sell on credit is to sell, not for immediate payment,

[1] The theory of desired cash balances, the sum of necessary and hoarded cash balances, is expounded in detail in *L'Ordre Social,* 3rd ed., p. 186.

but for a promise of payment at a later date, a promise which constitutes a claim to money.

The claim permits its holder to demand from the debtor, on maturity, the payment of the sum stipulated, and if the debtor defaults, to have recourse to means of recovery provided by law.

But the debtor can give only what he has. If he is unable or unwilling to reduce his cash balance, and if he does not expect to receive any money, he will honor his debt only if, when it falls due, he can sell goods of equal value: in other words, if he has at that date free capital assets in an equal amount.

The creditor may, of course, hope that his debtor will have some windfall. But as a rule, he will accept deferred payment only if, when the debt is contracted, the debtor possesses the capital assets needed to assure its settlement.

These assets may be expressly defined and immobilized, if the claim is secured. They are deposited in a suitable place, when the claim is a "warrant," or they may be blocked with a bank, if they are securities. In other cases, it may be a mortgage which assures the existence and the conservation of the assets that guarantee payment.

When the claim takes the form of a commercial bill, the "cause" of the claim is generally stated on the bill. It arises from the delivery of goods that will be kept among the assets of the debtor until the bill falls due and will represent, among these assets, the values that the debtor will realize for the liquidation of his debt.

If the claim is not secured, it is the total assets of the debtor or debtors that guarantee its payment.

All the guarantee procedures that are in force in practice —and especially the acceptance—are for the purpose of assuring the creditor that assets are in fact reserved to meet his claim and will be available, when it falls due, to assure settlement.

Thus, in almost all cases, under very diverse legal forms, the credit titles delivered in lieu of payment in a credit sales transaction represent an asset, defined or undefined, kept among the capital assets of the debtor with a view to its incorporation in a productive process or for reasons of expediency, but which is destined to be sold when the debt will have to be paid.

From this, it follows that a sale on credit may be considered, at the time when it is made, as an exchange between the thing bought and the wealth represented by the claim delivered in payment; that is to say, as a real act of barter.

The subject of the investigations that follow is the very diverse repercussions that the postponement of payment is capable of having on the equilibrium of markets where goods are exchanged for cash.

To simplify the analysis, we shall carry it out on the hypothesis of a situation in which the monetary stock of each individual remains constantly at the level of his desired cash balance, as a result of the fixity of the two magnitudes.

If, on this hypothesis, all transactions were settled in cash, the demand of each individual, in every market period, would be of the same amount as the supplies he offers; otherwise, his actual cash balance would not remain at the level of his desired cash balance.

If some transactions are settled by three-month bills, the situation must be examined at the time when the transaction occurs and at the time of its settlement.

At the time when the transaction is effected, the supplier receives a claim on the purchaser, but no payment. Since his actual cash balance is at the desired level, he cannot exercise a demand for anything. On his side, therefore, there has been supply without demand.

Inversely, the purchaser has no payment to make. He therefore has no need to supply anything in order to be able to demand.

The conclusion of the transaction on the basis of deferred settlement thus gives rise, on the part of the seller, to supply without a demand; on the part of the purchaser, to a demand unaccompanied by a supply. It therefore has no repercussion on the difference between total demand and total supply.

When the bill falls due, the debtor must settle with the

seller. Since his actual cash balance is at the level of his desired cash balance, he must supply something on the market, of the same value as his debt—a supply which is not accompanied by any demand.

Inversely, the creditor receives payment. If his cash balance is to remain unchanged, he must exercise a demand for a like amount, and thus he exercises a demand not offset by a supply.

Thus, the settlement of the deferred transaction will, likewise, not affect the difference between total demand and total supply.

A sale on credit, therefore, does not in itself have any disturbing effect; nor does it have any monetary repercussions. It is only a transfer during the life of the credit—i.e., a loan made by the seller to the purchaser—of the purchasing power which the former would have acquired from the proceeds of the sale if it had been made for cash.

But the seller may discount his claim.

If he sells it to the holder of an existing cash balance—and this is the case when he sells it, directly or indirectly, on the money market, when the latter is understood to be composed generally of others than banks (in French: marché hors-banque)—the purchaser of the claim, if he wishes to keep his actual cash balance at the level of his desired cash balance, will have to supply something on the market.

The seller of the claim, on his side, if he wishes to avoid an increase of his cash balance, will exercise a demand of the same amount.

Thus, once again, discounting a claim by selling it on the money market—i.e., a discount "outside the banks"—does not affect the difference between total demand and supply, and has no monetary repercussions. It merely transfers the loan arising from the credit, from the seller to the purchaser of the claim.

But the discounter may, directly or indirectly, transfer his claim to a bank (in French: escompte en banque). In that case, the situation is entirely changed.

The bank enters the claim among its assets and credits the

seller with an amount equal to the price at which it purchased the claim from the discounter. The liabilities of the bank are thus increased by the same amount.[1]

If the discounter is unwilling to enlarge his actual cash balance above the level of his desired cash balance, he will exercise a demand equal to the amount of the discount.

Thus, at the moment when a credit transaction is followed by a discount at a bank, we have on the side of the purchaser —as in the previous case—a demand without supply, and on the side of the seller, a demand to the value of his supply. There will thus be a net increase, by an amount equivalent to the value of the transaction effected—hence, by the amount of the cash balances newly created—in the difference between total demand and total supply.

When the credit becomes due, the beneficiary of the discount must repay the bank that made the discount. For this purpose, he must supply without demanding. From this it follows that the difference between total demand and total supply is reduced, by the increase of supply, to the extent that the difference between the total amount of actual cash balances and of desired cash balances has been reduced by reduction of the volume of money in circulation.

Thus, when the total amount of desired cash balances remains unaltered, discounting at a bank creates a disturbance characterized by a demand not offset by a supply at the moment when the discount is granted, and by a supply not offset by a demand when the debt is settled.

This disturbance, however, would not occur if the beneficiary of the discount were not to use the addition to his cash balances to exercise an additional demand on the market.

This will be the case, especially, if the discounting should coincide with additional business—arising, for instance, from

[1] If the bank is a bank of issue, the discount entails no further consequences for it. If it is a commercial bank, not enjoying the privilege of issuing legal tender, it may rediscount such claims with the Bank of Issue in an amount representing a fraction, generally a small one, of the sum by which its liabilities have been increased.

We shall not deal here with the consequences of such rediscounts, in order to avoid unnecessary complications.

an increase in employment—which would increase, by that amount, the total sum of cash balances required for settlements to be made. It will also be the case if the discounting were to coincide with an increase of the same amount in hoarded cash balances.

These two possibilities will thus affect in the same way, in the second member of the quantity equation, the total quantity of money in circulation and the total of desired cash balances; the difference between them will remain unchanged.

Thus, if discounting is not to cause a divergence between demand and supply, and therefore disturbance on the market, it is necessary and it is sufficient that the cash balances that it provides should be desired.

What is true in the case of an increase of discounting is true also, *mutatis mutandis,* for a reduction, by reimbursement, of bills previously discounted.

The preceding analysis allows us to penetrate further into the "miracles of credit."

The surprising feature, in the conclusion that has just been formulated, is that the discounting of a claim by a bank will not, if the money supplied by the discounting operation is "desired," increase total demand, even when the beneficiary of the discount uses the money he has obtained to exercise a demand on the market.

But to say that an additional sum of money is "desired" amounts to saying that, somewhere, one of the users of the monetary stock—who, as a general rule, is not the discounter —has increased, either the amount of his hoarded cash balances, or of the cash balances required by the settlements he has to make.

Now, all "hoarding" represents, to the extent of the amount involved, a postponement of re-spending; that is to say, it represents a supply—that which provided the hoarded money—not offset by a demand of the same amount.

Likewise, any increase in "necessary cash balances" reveals an increase in the quantity of money "in transit" for purposes of settlement. Now, money "in transit" is money which has been remitted by the purchaser, but not yet received by the seller. The purchaser obtained this money by supplying something. Other things being equal, he has therefore effected a supply and a demand of the same amount on the market. But on the hypothesis that all transactions are settled by cash payment, the seller will be able to exercise a demand equal to his supply only when he will have received the money remitted to him. He therefore consents to a delay in the re-spending of a like amount.

Thus, the fact that additional money is desired—either to increase hoarded cash balances, or to increase necessary cash balances—reveals that some participant in the market has brought about, to the extent of the amount involved, a supply unmatched by a demand.

This fact is often obscured by the circulation of money. It is indeed true that the postponement of re-spending ceases as soon as a part of the cash balances ceases to be "hoarded" or "necessary." Then this part of the cash balance is handed over to the seller. But if this part of the cash balance is still "desired," this means that some other participant in the market has increased his cash-balance requirements for the purpose of hoarding or settlement, and has thereby taken the place of the one who no longer desires some parts of his cash balance.

Thus, in a given market, the volume of postponements of re-spending—that is to say, of supplies not offset by demands of equal value—is always identically equal to the total amount of the desired cash balances.

It will be readily understood that the existence of these supplies not offset by demands, gives rise to the possibility of allowing, to the extent of the amount involved, a power to demand unaccompanied by supply, without giving rise to any disturbance; it is this power to demand which is given to those who discount bills with a bank, for the whole period the bills are outstanding.

But, in the phenomenon of discounting, there is no link between the persons who borrow and those who lend. The borrower is the debtor responsible for the discounted bill. The lender is the changing person who keeps among his assets the money arising from the discount, either as a hoarded cash balance or because, having sold nonmonetary goods, he is waiting for the settlement.

If the money arising from the discount were undesired, or if it should become so before the discounted bill falls due, the postponement of re-spending would cease. Then, if the discounted bill were to remain outstanding, the demand-without-supply that results from it would no longer be offset by the supply-without-demand resulting from the holding of desired cash balances. The discounting would bring about, either an enlargement of the volume of transactions, or a price rise, until such time as the money, no longer desired, is absorbed by the resulting enlargement of necessary cash balances.

The need for money creates, therefore, a possibility of making loans. But this possibility is strictly limited to the amount of the cash reserves actually desired. The corresponding possibility of making loans will apply to long-term loans or to short-term loans according to whether the need for cash balances is permanent or temporary. This is how it becomes possible to lend at long term, without adverse consequences, the counterpart of that residue of the circulation which is regarded as incompressible.

The mystery of credit is thus dispelled.

If the desire for money opens up a possibility of lending, this is because it reflects the decision of the person desiring the money to postpone its re-spending.

But if we wish to avoid the disorders arising from demands that are not offset by supplies—that is to say, the disorders from inflation—it is essential that the amount of loans made by way of *bank* discounts should never exceed the amount of desired cash balances, and, in particular, that it should be possible to reabsorb without delay discounts corresponding to the issues of money that have ceased to be desired.

This is why the central problem of monetary policy is that of maintaining, at all times, the volume of currency in circulation at the level of the total amount of desired cash balances.

We must now inquire by what methods this can be assured.

Influences regulating the amount of currency

It would seem to be generally admitted in our contemporary world that it is the monetary authorities who have the responsibility of watching over the quantity of money in circulation.

In France, a "Council of Credit" fixes the discount ceilings of the banks. In the United States, the monetary authorities alter the reserve percentages that the banks are required to keep. Everywhere, banks that create money are subject, by measures of law or of practice, to the wishes of the authorities who are responsible for credit policies.

Such institutional measures are only the reflection of the views, almost unanimous, of contemporary economists. These views are strongly expressed by Lord Keynes in his *General Theory of Employment, Interest and Money*.

In his opinion, the quantity of money in circulation is, in the hands of the monetary authorities, nothing but an instrument for directing economic activity. "If we are to control the activity of the economic system," he says, "by changing the quantity of money . . ." (p. 172).

And further on:

"The quantity of money," he says, "is not determined by the public. All that the propensity of the public toward hoarding can achieve is to determine the rate of interest at which the aggregate desire to hoard becomes equal to the available cash" (p. 174).

I do not contend, by any means, that the monetary authorities are, under all circumstances, incapable of influencing the quantity of currency in circulation. I can even imagine monetary systems under which they might have an absolute control over its issue. But I think that under the systems existing in Western Europe and in the United States, the users of money, by fixing the amount of their individual cash balances, exert a great influence on the total quantity of money in circulation, and that if their wishes in the matter can be frustrated, this is possible only in a certain direction and only when certain very special circumstances are realized. It seems to me, in addition, that by failing to state these conditions and by accepting the proposition that under all circumstances, the quantity of money depends solely on the market authorities, an omission is made which entails very serious consequences, both in the field of economic theory and in that of techniques capable of assuring the stability of prices.

My conviction is based on factual and on theoretic considerations.

First of all, I have the evidence of experience. As a member of the General Council of the Bank of France from 1936 to 1939, then as its Deputy Governor, I have often seen the Bank of Issue worried by variations in the currency circulation and trying to check them. I have found that, generally speaking, these variations conformed only in a small degree to its wishes. I seldom had the feeling that the Bank of Issue "caused variations" in the quantity of money.

As Director of the French Treasury (*Mouvement Général des Fonds*), I have known periods of deficit in which the circulation increased, and others, with an equal deficit, in which the circulation declined, without the authorities having taken any pains to bring about such movements and in spite of their efforts to thwart some of them.

The quantity of money in circulation is never anything but the total of the cash balances that all users of money keep in their tills or their note-case. Has it ever happened that any one of them has been prevented from increasing his cash balance when he wished to increase it, or from reducing it when he wished to reduce it?

The infallible method at the disposal of each of us, when we wish to increase our cash balance, is to buy less or to sell more—and if we wish to reduce it, to buy more and sell less.

If this is so, it means that each of us, in fixing the amount of its supplies or demands on the market, affects the volume of money in circulation, notwithstanding the wishes of the Issue Authorities except for special circumstances of which I shall speak further on.

The important thing that should, first of all, be ascertained is the mechanism through which the wishes of individuals affect the quantity of money in existence.

In attempting to do so, I shall study the mechanism through which the monthly variations in the monetary circulation are brought about. It is known that in all our countries this circulation increases regularly toward the end of the month and declines when once the period is over. It seems that the Bank of England brings about these variations systematically by the sale and purchase of Treasury bills on the market. The variations in the volume of money in circulation thus brought about by occurring ahead of needs, tend to avoid the variations in rates that these needs would otherwise cause. In France, since a recent date, the Bank of France can have recourse to the same practice. But previously, it did not do so, and yet the rhythm of the monthly variations occurred nonetheless, with the same amplitude and strict regularity, though no one made it his business to provoke them.

The very regularity of these variations suffices in itself to show the existence of a well defined "mechanism." It is its nature that I propose, in the first place, to investigate.

In order to analyze simply the process by which individual needs affect the quantity of money in circulation, I shall take the case of an isolated economy, i.e., one without international trade, and revolving, at the outset, in a regularly recurring way. The money, assumed to be inconvertible, is provided by the discounting of commercial bills or Treasury bills, each of the bills on maturity being replaced by a renewed bill of equal value.

I shall also assume the existence of a money market—a market composed of others than banks—on which the bills are bought and sold for money. I know that, in certain periods, this hypothesis did not correspond with reality. But the absence of a market composed of others than banks was due more to the state of the public finances than to permanent structural modifications. To have a market, there must be sellers and buyers. The permanent presence of a buyer willing to absorb all the money offered on the market evidently tends constantly to bring the market to the Bank and therefore to cause the disappearance of a market composed of others than banks. But if this special circumstance is weakened or disappears, a market composed of others than banks will tend to reappear, if, at first, only timidly and partially.

Toward the end of the month, the debtors, foreseeing the maturity of their obligations, wish to increase their cash holdings.

For this purpose they have no other resource that that of supplying without demanding.

The additional supplies, or the diminution of demands, cause prices to fall on the markets where they operate. Now, these additional supplies or diminutions of demands may concern either short-term bills (drafts or Treasury bills) or other forms of wealth (real wealth or long-term claims).

In the former case, the fall in the price of short-term bills is reflected in a rise in the rate of interest on the money market.

To simplify the analysis, I shall assume that the additional supplies and diminutions of demand are distributed over all market items in the same manner as are total supply and demand. This would be the case, especially, if every part of supply or demand were made up of an assortment of items having the same composition, for all the suppliers or demanders, in the market.

Then the excess of supplies and the restrictions of demands would entail simultaneously, and in a definite ratio, a rise in the short-term rate of interest and a fall in the general price level. The two movements would be indissolubly connected, as a consequence of the excess of supplies and the restriction of demands envisaged.

In practice, it may not work out this way. The excess of supplies or the restriction of demand will generally affect, in the first instance, the money market, which is more sensitive than the markets for real wealth or of long-term claims. But it can be shown that if one of the movements—either that of interest rates or of prices—occurs separately, it will have a tendency to draw the other after it.

The rise of short-term interest rates, for instance, should it occur without any change having taken place in the demand for real wealth, will make it advantageous to sell for cash under a repurchase agreement, and to invest in the money market, until the date of the settlement, the price of the purchase. This will lead to a fall in spot prices.

Inversely, the fall of spot prices, should it occur without any change having taken place in the demand for short-term bills, will make it advantageous to join a purchase for cash with a sale for future delivery, and to discount in the money market bills obtained from the sale, for the settlement of the purchase. And this will lead to a rise in interest rates on the money market.

If, under the existing systems, there were not enough short-term bills to provide, through discounts, the additional desired cash balances, then the prices of futures would rise relatively to spot prices. This would deflect supplies from the spot market to the market for futures. This, in its turn, would give rise to the additional bills required for providing the additional desired cash balances.

Thus, in all cases, desire for additional cash balances will tend to lower prices and raise short-term rates.

It is obvious that these results will occur only if "all conditions remain equal," and that if any special cause, such as the expectation of a price rise, should interfere, the fall in prices might be excluded, and only the rates would rise.

If, under a system working smoothly and without friction, the amplitude of the two connected movements would depend only on market conditions, in practice it will vary according to the nature of the initial impulse—supply of real wealth or supply of bills—and according to the degree of sensitiveness of the various markets. Generally speaking, the money market will be the first to be affected.

But the two movements—the movement of prices and the movement of interest rates—whatever be the ratio between them, will combine to provide, through the mechanism expounded below, the additional desired cash balances.

The fall in prices will reduce the amount of cash balances needed for the settlement of transactions. By so doing, it will set free the money required to provide additional cash balances.

Should the rate on the money market, in spite of its rise, remain below the discount rate, then the additional desired cash balances will be supplied by reduction of necessary cash balances consequent on the fall of prices.

But if the market rate is, around the middle of the month, generally lower than the discount rate, the rise in the former, toward the end of the month, will have the effect of bringing it closer to the latter.

Now, as soon as the former attains the level of the latter, it ceases to rise, and the Bank of Issue "takes"—directly or indirectly—all the bills offered for which there is no demand at that rate on the market.

But whenever a bank buys a bill it creates money.

From this, it follows that, as soon as the market rate has hit the level of the discount rate, the additional cash balances which are still desired are provided entirely by the money created in exchange for the bills sold to the Bank. The fall in prices ceases, at the same time as the rise in interest rates.

The sooner the market rate reaches the level of the discount rate—or, to state it otherwise, the closer the latter is to the former—the quicker the process of monetization comes into play, and the smaller will be the price fall consequent upon a like increase of desired cash balances.

When settlement day has passed, the inverse phenomenon comes into play, but in a manner which makes it a little more complex.

In such cases, the fact of a diminution in the payments to be effected makes some parts of cash balances undesired.

Their holders have then only one means of getting rid of them: namely, that of demanding without supplying.

As has been shown above, their demand may affect the short-term bills market or the market for other forms of wealth.

But each day, as a result of the maturing of bills previously discounted, bills created for renewal—we are assuming that the economy revolves in a regularly recurring way —have to be discounted.

Now, during the month-end market sessions, as long as additional cash balances were desired, the renewal bills offered on the market were brought "to the bank" to be monetized there.

The additional demand for bills on the money market reduces, by a corresponding amount, the amount of bills discounted by the banks.

But each time that a discount made by a bank is replaced by a discount made by someone other than a bank, the quantity of money in circulation is reduced by that amount.

As long as the total demand for bills remains lower than the supply of bills on the market, the market rate will remain at the level of the rate of discount.

As soon as, at a market session, the demand for bills exceeds the amount of the previous discounts becoming due, and therefore the amount of the renewal bills presented on the market, the demand for bills will exceed the supply. The total volume of renewal bills will be sold on the market, but it will not suffice to reabsorb the whole of the undesired cash balances.

Then the market rate will fall below the rate of discount, and the level of spot prices will begin to rise.

From this moment on, it is through the increase of cash balances necessary for the settlement of transactions that the residue of cash balances remaining undesired will be absorbed.

This shows that in the absence of resales, on the market, of unmatured bills, i.e., of open-market operations, the amount of the maturities of bills previously discounted constitutes, at each market session, the limit of possible reabsorption of undesired cash balances.

It is to assure a minimum of daily maturities, and thereby a minimum of elasticity in the currency circulation, that most monetary systems have been led to limit the duration of bills accepted for discount.

However, it may happen that the discount rate is fixed at so low a level that it is constantly below the equilibrium rate, in the market exclusive of banks.

In such a case, there is a constant flow of discounting at the bank and a constant increase in the quantity of money in circulation.

But the existence of undesired cash balances increases spot prices relatively to the prices of futures. This deflects offers from the futures markets to the spot markets and leads to the reduction of commercial portfolios, which is characteristic of all inceptions of inflation.

Now, every substitution of a spot sale for a futures sale leads, if the bill relating to the futures sale was discounted by a bank, to the payment of the matured bill, and therefore, by a corresponding amount, to the reabsorption of money.

This shows that in all those cases in which discounted bills represent real wealth, which can be sold for spot as well as for future delivery, a lasting inflation is not possible. The inflationary process can develop only during the intermediary period that separates the disturbance from the displacement that tends to correct it. The sooner the latter follows the former, the less extreme will be the disturbance, and the more rapidly will equilibrium be re-established.

And here let it not be said that the mechanism of creation and reabsorption of money we have just analyzed is purely theoretical. All market operators know how sensitive rates are and how quickly they react to the influences affecting them.

In practice, it is true, appearances are complicated by the interference of several mechanisms that have their point of departure or arrival not only in money, but also in international exchanges or in the production and consumption of gold. We shall present a brief summary view of this matter in our section on the equilibrium of the balance of payments.

However, in the monthly variations of the quantity of money in circulation, the variation in desired cash balances is, generally speaking, the dominant causal factor. The switching of demands for discounting either toward the nonbank market or toward the banks, according to whether the providing of money is greater or less than the total amount of desired cash balances, offers a very clear confirmation of the preceding analysis.

It shows that the discount rate is, in a certain sense, the threshold beyond which increases in desired cash balances are met by the creation of new money rather than by the lowering of prices, and that the nearer the discount rate is to the market rate, the better chance there is that the general price level will be stable.

The convertibility of notes into gold or into foreign bills complicates the mechanism, by adding to variations in the general price level the possibility of variations in monetary reserves. Here again it is in the section dealing with international exchanges that we shall indicate the consequences of the option to which this gives rise.

Inflation

The preceding analysis throws light on the mechanism of inflation.

The state of deficit is characterized by the existence of demands that the would-be demander cannot or will not cover by supplies of an equal amount, nor by reducing his cash balances.

He tries to procure resources by offering on the market securities—generally Treasury bills—which he undertakes to redeem at maturity. But when he does not have the resources necessary for such redemption, the arrival of the due date forces him to offer only a renewal bill, in the same amount as that which has fallen due, which is added to those arising from the current deficit.

Thus, the volume of bills offered on the market will increase steadily. There will therefore, necessarily, come a moment, at the beginning of a deficit period, when the market's capacity to absorb Treasury bills will be exhausted.

At this moment, in order to avoid suspending payments, the State, by measures of law or administration, compels the banks, and especially the Bank of Issue, to take all bills offered that are not demanded by the market.

But in taking the undesired Treasury bills, the banks create additional cash balances that, if all conditions remain unchanged, are undesired. Then the process of reabsorption, described in the preceding section, comes into play.

The holders of undesired cash balances exert a demand for additional bills. Market rates fall, as is observed at the beginning of all periods of inflation. It is the well-known circuit phenomenon, by which the volume of Treasury bills absorbed by the market keeps on increasing as the deficit increases.

But, generally speaking, the additional demand for bills amounts to only a fraction of the deficit; therefore, should the deficit continue, the supply of claims, on the market outside of the banks, rapidly exceeds the demand. As soon as this is the case, the rate in the market outside of the banks "sticks" to the discount rate, and as has been noted in all countries where there is a permanent deficit, the market outside the banks disappears.

That portion of the bills arising out of the deficit that is not taken up by the market is taken by the banks. The holders of undesired cash balances thus created, not wishing to hold claims, demand real wealth: goods or services.

Spot quotations rise relatively to futures quotations. Sales of futures diminish.

Here again experience confirms the theory with great rigor. At the beginning of every period of inflation, we observe a characteristic diminution of all commercial portfolios.

The disadvantageous character of sales of futures leads to the repayment of all bills susceptible of being repaid, i.e., of all those with regard to which the debtor enjoys a real option as between a spot transaction and a futures transaction.

But the repayment of a bill previously discounted at a bank leads to the reabsorption of money, and therefore to a reduction in the amount of undesired cash balances. It thereby suppresses or reduces the inflation by a corresponding amount.

The process of shifting offers of real wealth from term to spot transactions may be accelerated and amplified by raising the rate at which the bank take bills for discount.

We have seen, indeed, that as soon as the supply of bills permanently exceeds the demand in the market outside of the banks, the market rate gets to be on a level with the discount rate. By raising the latter—generally by raising the rate of the Bank of Issue—the cost of discounting is increased.[1] This induces the holders of the wealth—which is to be used either for transformation in a productive process or as inventories —to sell this wealth for cash rather than on account, and therefore to repay at maturity the bills that represented this wealth.

If the Bank of Issue always had among its assets, as a counterpart of the money it creates, some assets which could be sold on the market at the price at which they had been monetized, all undesired cash balances could be reabsorbed. There could be inflation only to the extent that, and during the periods in which, the mechanism of reabsorption would not have been operating.

This would be the case, in particular, if the Treasury bills were only an anticipation of fiscal receipts expected from the sale of public services. All the Government would then have to do would be to advance the date fixed for the collection of its taxes, or to induce tax-payers to pay in advance—as is now

[1] It is this rise in the discount rate, generally occurring when the rate outside of the banks "sticks" to the discount rate, that leads people to consider inflation periods as periods of dear money. It is evident that during such periods the additional demands exercised by the holders of undesired cash balances are directed more toward real wealth than toward short-term claims. Then the inverse solidarity of price movements and movements of interest rates, discussed in the previous section, may be affected.

done in France and in other countries—by abatements on the amount of advance payments. Then the repayment of bills previously discounted would assure the reabsorption of cash balances no longer desired. Then all inflation could be avoided.

But what characterizes a state of deficit is that a Treasury bill is only in appearance a claim. The issuer has no option as between repayment or renewal. Every demand for repayment compels him only to increase, by a corresponding amount, his offers of bills on the market.

Consequently, as soon as all the true claims that have been discounted have been reimbursed, or rather as soon as that portion of these claims for which the debtors have a true option as between reimbursement and renewal is exhausted, the mechanism that tends to reabsorb undesired cash balances becomes inoperative. Their holders, in order to get rid of them, exercise a demand for real wealth without their demand leading, through the rise of spot quotations relatively to futures quotations, to the supply of such real assets on the market.

Then, as the result of the excess of total demand over the total value of supplies, the general price level begins to rise. This rise of the price level, by increasing the volume of cash balances needed for the settlement of transactions, absorbs the quantities of nonreasorbable money arising from the discounting of undesired fictitious claims.

A state of inflation exists.

From this point on, all increases in the discount rate are powerless to cause the substitution of spot sales for futures. Such increases act only to the limited extent to which it may increase the demand for claims on the part of holders of undesired cash balances.

Moreover, the expectation of a price rise maximizes the desire to accumulate inventories, and therefore to discount for speculative purposes. It intensifies the demand for real assets, but at the same time discourages the supply of such assets. It tends therefore to intensify inflationary pressure.

Against this pressure, monetary maneuvers are practically useless.

Thus, for a state of inflation to develop, it is not sufficient that the quantity of money in circulation should exceed the total amount of desired cash reserves; it is also indispensable that this money should be issued against securities that are not redeemable on maturity, i.e., against fictitious claims.

As long as there exists among the assets of Banks of Issue a crust of securities representing values that can be sold for cash as well as on account, i.e., true values, the surplus money will tend to be reabsorbed as a result of the compression of commercial portfolios. But as soon as these portfolios have fallen to a level below which they cannot go—the bills composing them having been issued solely with a view to encashment, or being capable only of renewal, and not of repayment, because the debtor does not possess capital assets—then there is no influence which is capable of reabsorbing the undesired cash balances.

Then, money is no longer anything but a nominal token, with no counterpart of equal value. Its quantity no longer depends on anything but the deficit and the demand by savers for the bills representing the deficit. All "mechanisms" are blocked.

It is from this moment only that we have the situation implicitly admitted into the whole Keynesian construction. It is then, only, that the mechanism described in the *General Theory* becomes an exact image of reality, and at the same time full validity is given to the prescription for economic and monetary policy proceeding from that theory as the sole means for controlling inflation.

The parable of the dinner

For the matter with which we are dealing, the parable of the dinner has extreme theoretical importance. Now, the preceding analysis throws new light on it.

"An act of individual saving means—so to say— a decision

not to have dinner to-day . . . Thus it depresses the business of preparing today's dinner without stimulating the business of making ready for some act of future consumption" (*General Theory of Employment, Interest, and Money*, p. 210).

The thesis could apply only—this goes without saying—to savings that remain unspent. But even in this narrow form, it cannot be regarded as entirely correct.

An individual act of saving, which reflects the decision not to dine today, entails, if it is not followed by any additional investment, an increase of "hoarded cash balances." It thereby sets in motion the regulatory process described above.

As long as the rate in the market outside of the banks has not attained the level of the discount rate, there are indeed supplies without demands. The reduction of the volume of transactions or the price fall resulting therefrom the "necessary cash balances" and thereby releases the desired additional amounts of money. The parable of the dinner gives an accurate description of reality.

But as soon as the market rate hits the level of the discount rate—and, in fact, since one is always close to the other, this happens quickly—the mechanism becomes very different.

Debtors on matured bills previously discounted in the market outside of the banks are led to discount renewal bills "at the bank."

Now, discounting at a bank represents supply outside of the market. The purchase of bills to which it gives rise is made not against funds already in existence, but against money newly created.

As for the bill discounted—unless it be a Treasury bill issued to finance a deficit—it represents values included among the assets of the debtors, at some point of the economic circuit.

Everything proceeds as if the decision not to dine today had led to placing in reserve outside the market, among the assets of the banking system, wealth equivalent to that whose consumption is deferred by the refusal to dine.

In exchange for this wealth, the discounting bank has

delivered a deposit receipt, which constitutes money. By so doing, it has increased the quantity of existing money and has provided the additional cash balances desired by the economic subject who renounced his dinner.

Thus, the act of saving will not have generated depression. By increasing the amount of desired cash balances, it will actually have opened, in the assets of money-creating banks, outlets of an equal amount. The latter will have, as counterpart, an equivalent increase of wealth as inventory or kept within the productive process with a view to future consumption.

Inversely, at the time when the investor decides to dine, he will reduce the amount of his desired cash balance by the price of his meal. Through the regulating mechanism analyzed above, the quantity of money in circulation will tend to diminish by an equal amount. This diminution will result from the repayment of a bank discount which has matured, either through its replacement by a discount outside the banks or by the substitution of a cash sale for a sale on account.

In the first case, the bill that renews the matured one will have been sold on the market, while that which it replaced was held, outside the market, among the assets of the money-creating bank. The total supply of nonmonetary wealth—which includes claims representing real wealth as that wealth itself—will be increased by a corresponding amount.

In the second case, the substitution of a cash transaction for a sale on account will compel the purchaser to repay the matured bill and therefore to sell on the market the resources that were its counterpart among his assets. The repayment of the bill discounted at the bank reduces by that amount the quantity of money in circulation.

Everything proceeds as if the saver, when deciding to dine, had induced some one of the users of money to withdraw from the vaults of the bank the wealth that had been deposited there when he missed his meal, so as to offer it for sale on the market. To obtain this wealth, he presents the deposit receipt that constitutes the money created at the time when the saving was made.

Thus, the decision to dine creates no more disturbance than did the decision not to dine. It only brings back on the market wealth that had been put aside to meet such a contingency, while it destroys the monetary tokens by which that wealth had been represented.

This same analysis holds good, *mutatis mutandis,* for an act of saving that consists in the conservation of the proceeds of an unspent loan, and for the act of investment or consumption that its utilization entails.

In the special case in which the borrowed wealth consists of gold previously hoarded, the working of the mechanism is even more directly perceptible. If it is the State that borrows, it gives the lender a loan certificate and remits the gold to its Bank of Issue. The latter, in turn, opens for the State a credit of an equal amount.[1]

As long as the proceeds of the loan are not spent, the State increases, by a corresponding amount, the cash balance that it holds. There is, therefore, no effect on total demand.

When the State uses the resources obtained from the loan to exercise a demand, the increase in demand resulting therefrom tends to bring about, through the mechanism just described, a reabsorption of money, i.e., an offer, on the market, equivalent to the wealth that represented, in the portfolio of the issuing banks, the counterpart of the money reabsorbed.

The equilibrium of the balance of payments

The preceding analysis enables us to describe more accurately the mechanism that tends to assure equilibrium in international obligations. By showing the limits of this mech-

[1] If the holder of gold had been paid in money, the option would be the same: maintenance of an increased cash balance as long as the proceeds of the sale of the gold were not spent, or an increase of demand tending to reduce the quantity of money in circulation afterwards.

anism, it rectifies the oversimplified picture that is generally given of it.

To simplify the exposition, I shall assume that gold is concentrated among the assets of the banking system and cannot be withdrawn therefrom—except for making foreign settlements. I shall also suppose, as in the previous sections, that for each participant in the market, his actual cash balance is at the level of his desired cash balance.

If, at a given market session, the balance of international payments is in deficit, this means that the amount of settlements to be made to foreign countries exceeds that of the settlements expected from such countries.

The purchase of the means of transfer necessary for settling the deficit is effected at banks, and therefore outside the market. It entails a twofold consequence:

With respect to total market equilibrium, it gives rise to a supply without a demand, since the individual seeking gold or foreign exchange must, in order to secure them, offer on the market either real wealth or claims, but he exercises outside the market the demand that is the counterpart of this supply; with respect to money, it gives rise to the reabsorption of the quantity of money brought to the bank in exchange for the gold or foreign exchange requested.

The supply-without-demand causes a fall in prices if it involves real wealth; it raises interest rates if it involves claims.

If we admit, as in the preceding sections, that the two movements are indissolubly associated, they may bring about all or some of the three following reactions:

a. Increase of exports resulting from the fall of domestic prices relatively to foreign prices. Now, the foreign purchaser, in order to settle for his purchase, makes a supply on his own market. His action therefore gives rise to a demand-without-supply, which re-establishes total market equilibrium, while the settlement for his purchases tends to bring the actual circulation back to the level of the total amount of desired cash balances;

b. Increase of the domestic output of gold, resulting from

the fall in the cost of production of an article—gold—which is the only one on the market that is sold at a fixed price to the Central Bank. Now, the sale of gold to the Central Bank is a sale outside the market, whereas the purchase of the services that produced the gold is made on the market. The resulting demand-without-supply itself tends to re-establish total market equilibrium and to bring the actual circulation back to the total level of the desired cash balances;

    c. Increase of discounts at the banks, as soon as the market rate reaches the level of the discount rate. This increase in discounts at the banks means, for the discounter, the return of the new monetary units that were created as the reception of discounting by the banks. Since his desired cash balance is assumed to be at the level of his actual cash balance, he increases his demand on the market by a corresponding amount.

The resulting demand-without-supply re-establishes the total market equilibrium, while the creation of new money brings the actual circulation back to the total level of desired cash reserves.

This third procedure has the effect of replacing, in the balances sheet of the banking system, some gold or foreign bills by short-dated paper in terms of local currency. It reduces, by a corresponding amount, the percentage of cover for the currency.

It is indeed by means of one of these three procedures that the regulating mechanism will re-establish the equilibrium of the balance of payments. The first two will establish a condition of regular recurrence, and therefore one which is capable of lasting indefinitely; the third will progressively reduce the reserves of the banking system.

Now, the degree of switching from one to another of these three possible procedures will depend on the elasticity of exports, the domestic cost of producing gold, and on the position of the discount rate relatively to the rate outside the banks.

Everything takes place as though the means necessary for the re-establishment of equilibrium could be drawn from three distinct sources: foreign trade, gold buried in the ground, gold and foreign bills buried in the reserves of the banking system. Access to each of them is gained over a threshold placed at a certain level. It is the first one to be reached which provides, in fact, the resources which will re-establish equilibrium.

If we assume that the cost of newly extracted gold is high, the choice between the re-establishment of equilibrium by an increase of exports or a reduction of imports, on the one hand, or by drawing on convertible reserves, on the other, will depend, other things being equal with respect to the elasticity of international transactions, on the level of the discount rate relatively to the rate outside the banks, at the particular point of time under consideration.

This shows the importance of the level of the discount rate. By moving it away from the rate outside the banks, we raise the threshold that allows recourse to the reserves of the Bank of Issue. We thereby increase the chances of re-establishing equilibrium in international transactions.

We see, at the same time, that the deficit, which creates undesired cash reserves, by making the market rate "stick" to the discount rate in the banks, gives immediate access to the reserves of the banking system for re-establishing equilibrium in international transactions. It thereby practically excludes all possibility of re-establishing this equilibrium by increasing exports or reducing imports.

The New Commandment of austerity

Our fathers would have been very much astonished had they been told that it might be their duty, one day, not only to reduce their expenditures to the level of their resources, but not to spend the money they had laboriously earned.

Such a commandment would have been inconceivable to them.

As a rule, their monetary resources arose from the sale of wealth of equal value. The demand which they exercised in using these resources was justified economically, as well as ethically, by a contribution of equal value that they had made to the market, and therefore could not cause a disturbance of any kind in that market.

If the resources by means of which they exercised their demand arose, not from a sale of real wealth or of claims on the market, but from a discount which the prevailing level of rates had brought "into the banks," rather than on the market outside banks, or, in other words, if their purchase was financed by money newly created, this means that some money-user had increased the cash balance that he wished to retain, and therefore had wished to postpone the use of the power to re-spend which it afforded him.

It is true that the equivalent of the wealth which this user temporarily renounced had been "parked" in a bank, ready to be placed again on the market when, as a result of a reduction of his desired cash balance, the postponement of the re-spending would end.

If the purchaser meant to pay for his purchase by drawing on his own cash balance—for instance, by spending the proceeds of previous saving or of a previous loan—then his demand, not offset by a supply, led to the return to the market of wealth against which the cash balances, no longer desired, had been created. There, again, the total equilibrium of the market was preserved.

Thus, in all cases, disturbances could be only limited, because they were reduced to those that would arise from the time elapsing between the monetary adjustments and the inducements that tended to cause them.

Under such conditions, it is unthinkable that a policy of austerity might have been necessary.

But the situation was completely changed when an important part of existing money was issued against claims that did not have as their counterpart, among the assets of the debtor, wealth of equal value.

In those days, when the "crust" of real values—i.e., of values capable of being sold at the price at which they had been monetized—existing in the portfolios of money-creating banks was exhausted, it was sufficient to effect the slightest reduction in the amount of desired cash balances—caused, for example, by the utilization of a loan heretofore unspent, by the emergence of a deficit in international transactions, or by recourse to bank discounts unmatched by a like increase in the amount of desired cash balances—to cause a general rise in the price level, i.e., an inflationary phenomenon, unless indeed these changes did not bring about an equivalent increase in the volume of transactions.

The only means then available for avoiding or mitigating inflationary disorders was to prevent, by admonition or compulsion, the exercising of demand without counterpart—that is to say, the equivalent of those demands that sought their financing, not through the offering of supplies of equal value, but through the utilization of cash balances already in existence.

Thus, it is only when the portfolios of money-creating banks no longer contain a cushion of true claims, capable of meeting all foreseeable variations in the quantity of money in circulation, that a policy of austerity may become necessary.

But it is a grave error to see in such a policy the product of economic fatality, or the result of an inevitable modification of economic structures. What makes it necessary is that money has really become what Keynes implicitly supposed it to be, i.e., a mere token, unmatched in the assets of Banks of Issue by any counterpart of realizable values.

To avoid ever having to face the possibility of recourse to a policy of austerity, it is sufficient that any quantity of currency that has become unnecessary should be reabsorbed by realizing on the market an equivalent amount of assets of the Bank of Issue. The sooner it will be reabsorbed, the less will be the transitory disturbances to which the change of monetary conditions will have given rise.

The institutional problem
of money

Contrary to the belief of the uninformed, there is no orthodoxy in monetary matters. A great number of systems can be conceived, each of which has its own distinctive merits. It is only from the standpoint of the functions that one assigns to Society that any one of these systems may seem preferable to the others.

At present, the consensus demands, above all, of a monetary system that it should not hinder the development of production, and should thereby favor the "full employment" of productive possibilities, but at the same time it wishes that the system chosen should give to the general price level the fullest stability consistent with the preceding aim.

We have seen that the growth of production, by increasing the amount of "necessary" cash balances, increases by the same amount the desired cash balances. In order to reduce to a minimum the variations in the general price level related to variations in the amount of desired cash balances, it is necessary and it is sufficient that the quantity of money in circulation be adjusted, as quickly and as accurately as possible, to variations in the total amount of desired cash balances.

In the present state of affairs, with respect to the demands of our social conscience, it is essentially this quality that the monetary system should develop to the maximum.

The two extreme types of monetary systems are: the "realist" under which each unit of money has, as a counterpart in the balance-sheet of the bank which has issued it, an asset that can be sold on the market for an equal value; and the "nominalist," under which money is nothing but a token, void of substance. All the systems that have been, are, or will be in force range somewhere between these two models.

The essential feature of the "realist" system is that, if

suitably administered, it permits the creation of a situation that tends to avoid all threats of inflation or deflation.

If, indeed, the amount of actual cash balances should fall below the total amount of desired cash balances, all a bank needs to do is to purchase on the market real wealth, or claims, thereby creating new cash balances that will tend to avoid a state of deflation.

Inversely, should the amount of actual cash balances be higher than the total amount of desired cash balances, the issuing bank has only to sell some of its assets on the market— either real wealth or claims—in order to reabsorb the undesired cash balances.

Nevertheless, in the case in which it sells claims, a possible complication has to be faced. The supply of such claims tends to raise the rate in the market outside of the banks. Should this rate reach the level of the discount rate, the additional supply of claims will not reduce the total amount of claims discounted at banks, but will only replace, by new discounts at banks, the claims sold by the banks. The sale of claims will not suffice to reabsorb the undesired cash balances.

To assure their disappearance, if the discount rate is not at a higher level than the equilibrium rate on the market outside the banks, whatever it may be, the bank must refuse to discount the claims offered to it—which amounts to raising the bank rate to an infinite level. This will then compel the suppliers of claims, who will be unable to sell them on the market, to substitute cash sales for sales on account, in order to employ the means they obtain from the former for the repayment of the discounts to which the latter had given rise.

In this way, undesired cash balances can always be reabsorbed, provided that the money be actually a "realist" money —in other words, a true money—under which there will exist, behind each bill discounted, true values capable of being sold for cash on the market. When such a situation exists—and even as long as there exists among the assets of banks of issue a "crust" of truly realizable values—a permanent inflation can arise only if these institutions do not sell the assets whose, in being sold, would have reabsorbed the undesired cash balances.

Nevertheless, in the preceding analysis, the operations called for in order to avoid possible deflationary or inflationary tendencies, are either open-market operations or measures for the quantitative control over the volume of discounts. They call for systematic intervention on the part of the Banks of Issue. Now, all practitioners know the difficulty met with in foreseeing inflationary or deflationary tendencies before they produce their effects. Therefore, more or less intentionally, monetary systems have been so devised that the regulating reactions have a tendency to develop spontaneously, thus acquiring a partially self-regulating character.

These regulatory reactions are always based on the utilization of the reactions which any state of deflation or inflation tends to bring about, both on the scale of prices, and, while this is changing, on rates in the money market.

In order to utilize shifts in the scale of prices, the monetary unit is defined as a given quantity of a given form of wealth—generally, gold—and the Bank of Issue is required to purchase at a fixed price all quantities of metal supplied and not demanded, and to sell at a fixed price all quantities of gold demanded but not supplied.

The lowering of the price scale tends to raise the quantity of the metal offered on the market, either because it produces a surplus in the balance of international payments or because it increases the production of gold, the only form of wealth that, in periods of deflation, still has unlimited markets at an unchanging price. The increase in the Bank's purchases of gold provides the additions to the desired cash balances.

However, these variations in the supply of gold are relatively slow, although those which arise from variations in the balance of international payments are quicker than those that arise from changes in the rate of gold extraction. To increase the sensitiveness of self-regulating mechanisms, one uses the fact that any movement in prices, while in progress, tends to produce, if other conditions remain the same, an inverse movement in rates outside of the banks. Therefore, the Bank of Issue is required, when rates reach a certain level, to buy all sound short-term claims which are offered and for which there is no demand.

This arrangement is not analogous to that which a bimetallic system would establish, for the money price of a claim, other things being equal, moves with the price scale. It tends merely to limit the rise of a magnitude which varies, not in inverse proportion to the general price level, but in inverse proportion to the derivative (in French mathematical language: la dérivée) of the variations of the price level with respect to time.

The obligation for the bank to buy, at a certain rate, all claims supplied and not demanded, does not have the same effect as metallic convertibility—which is to prevent a fall in the scale of prices below the level corresponding to the monetary parity—but tends to restrain declines in the scale of prices as soon as the rate outside the banks reaches the level of the discount rate, whatever the price level may be at that time.

The two mechanisms—convertibility into gold, convertibility into claims—superimpose their effects, the second tending to check downward movements, the first tending to bring the scale of prices back to the level established by the convertibility rate.

It goes without saying that the second mechanism may be put into effect without the first. We shall show, further on, with what results.

Under such a system, inflation would produce—*mutatis mutandis*—inverse reactions.

However, here the mechanism is a little more complicated, since it must tend no longer to introduce securities into the balance sheet of the Banks of Issue, but to get rid of them. Now, a discounted bill normally remains in the portfolio of the bank that has discounted it until the maturity date, which is the only time when, regardless of the variations in discount rates since it was discounted, it attains its nominal value. Moreover, if at any moment it may be removed from the portfolio of the bank by an open-market operation, it is only at the time of renewal, i.e., at the maturity date, that it necessarily gives rise to an option between discounting the renewal bill at a bank and discounting it outside the banks. It is therefore only up to the amount of the daily maturities of bills already discounted that a monetary system presents each day a self-regulating tendency to contraction. The higher this amount and, therefore, the shorter the term of the bills discounted, the more elasticity does the circulation acquire in a downward sense. Indeed, it is in order to assure a minimum of elasticity in a downward sense, and not for the reasons usually adduced—such as the normal length of the commercial cycle—that the statutes of Banks of Issue limit to three months the term of paper eligible for discount.

A circulation based on the discount of long-term paper retains a spontaneous elasticity in an expansionist direction. On the other hand, in the direction of contraction, although it is still capable of regulation by open-market operations, it would be self-regulating only in small degree. It would cease to be self-regulating altogether if the paper had no maturity date at all.

"Nominalist" money consists of tokens without intrinsic value, lacking any realizable counterpart in the balance sheet of the bank that issued it.

Such money can be brought into circulation by a deficit and withdrawn by a surplus. It will therefore never be self-regulating, and can be regulated only by the utilization of an appropriate fiscal policy.

With respect to it, the management rules of the Keynesian pharmacopaeia will have to be used.

However, in our times, no money has ever presented all the characteristics of a monetary nominalism, but only some of them, as a result of a perversion of convertible systems originating in deficit.

Indeed, monetary realism has one essential consequence: It forbids expenditure which is not offset by the relinquishment of an equal value. If it permits to advance the monetization of an asset, it excludes a deficit.

For this reason, regimes that cannot or will not renounce

a deficit, have suspended, in their own favor, the fundamental rule of monetary realism, by forcing their Bank of Issue to accept for discount claims in the form of Treasury bills that in the absence of foreseeable receipts, they did not have means of redeeming.

This regime was not one of a pure monetary nominalism, for it preserved the outward forms of realism, by making the creation of monetary units subject to the delivery of a claim of equal value. But it lacked the fundamental characteristic of monetary realism: the "reality" of the claims eligible for discount.

Such a regime opened, for the party that benefited thereby—usually the State—the door to a deficit. To the extent to which the State used this opening, it offered Treasury bills, similar in form to true claims. All those that were not demanded by the market were taken by the banking system. The discount of these bills created, in an equal amount, additional cash balances, generally undesired. But the holders of these undesired cash balances were not willing to demand Treasury bills, for if they had been, the bills would have been demanded in the market outside the banks and would not have been brought "into the banks." The holders of undesired cash balances therefore demanded real assets, thus leading, through the mechanism analyzed above, to the substitution of cash sales for sales on account. But as soon as the portfolio representing true values—generally the short-term commercial portfolio—had been reduced to a minimum below which it could not fall, the mechanism operated without effect. The excess of demand did not lead to a supply, on the market, of wealth "parked" in the bank—for such wealth no longer existed—but only to a rise of prices. Inflation began, and nothing—except a fiscal surplus—could have made it possible to ward it off.

Thus, the eligibility of false claims for discount creates a regime which continues to be self-regulating in the direction of expansion, but ceases to be so in the direction of contraction as soon as the volume of portfolios of true claims, among the assets of the banking system, is reduced to a minimum below which it cannot fall.

The preceding analysis defines the conditions which a monetary system must satisfy if it is to be capable of checking inflation.

The fundamental condition—without which the money which the system provides is a lifeless body acted on only by the impulses transmitted to it from outside—is to admit to monetization only true assets, i.e., assets that can be sold on the market for the value at which they have been monetized.

It should be pointed out, however, that this condition may be mitigated, without doing any harm, because, in order to enable a monetary system to ward off any possible inflation it is sufficient that there be in the portfolios of all Banks of Issue a "crust" of real values sufficient to reabsorb all that part of the currency issue that is capable of becoming undesired. There is therefore no objection to the acceptance of perpetual or very long-term paper for the whole of the incompressible residue of the monetary circulation.

It will be said that to limit eligibility for discount to bills of genuine value is to assume that the problem has been solved; since, in order for the Government to be able to renounce the discounting of fictitious claims, its budget must be balanced and, inversely, if the budget should be balanced, the Government will not present fictitious claims to be discounted, even if they were eligible for discount.

But such an objection forgets that the problem of the deficit is as much a psychological as a financial one. To refuse to incur a deficit when one knows it can be financed by the issue of fictitious claims, is an act of reason, whereas if fictitious claims are ineligible for discount, it is the result of the impossibility of doing so.

It is true that fictitious claims can always be made eligible for discount. But then this entails the renunciation of currency convertibility. Now, public opinion knows, from experience, the consequences of the suspension of convertibility. Governments will resign themselves to it only when the very existence of the country is at stake, that is to say, in case of war.

Moreover, when false claims are ineligible for rediscount, in the Central Bank, all banking institutions are obliged, under threat of endangering their own solvency, to refuse to discount claims that have no intrinsic value. When the currency is convertible, the Central Bank itself is subjected to the same discipline, for the same reason. Thus, it is not legal obligations, but actual necessities—much more imperious—that tend to preserve a regime of true money.

Should it be desired, in addition, to give to the monetary system a self-regulating character in both directions, it is sufficient to limit the maturity of bills eligible for rediscount. The Central Bank of Issue, in laying down the requirements for the paper it will accept for rediscounting, will impose the necessary discipline on all other banks.

Lastly, by means of its rate of discount, the Central Bank will determine, under a system of convertibility, the composition of the reserves that it will hold against money in circulation. It will determine, especially, the amount of its reserves in gold or foreign bills, and thereby, the volume of credit it will grant to the economy in addition to that resulting from savings.

In concluding this study, the problem of monetary control is seen as follows:

A nominalist currency, as well as a currency that has as its counterpart, on the balance sheets of the Banks of Issue, only fictitious claims, must be controlled in its amount if it is desired to avoid the disorders of inflation. "Quantitative" control of credit will be a necessity in this case.

On the other hand, a realist currency can always be controlled by open-market operations. Even these operations will be useless if the currency is made sufficiently self-regulatory by limiting the maturity of bills accepted for discount. In any of these two cases, no quantitative control will be necessary. The only duty of the issuing authorities, i.e., of the banks, will be to watch over the real quality of the claims which they accept for discount, and therefore over the solvency of their debtors. Here again, the private banks will be led to take this precaution if the Central Bank imposes it on itself. The control, indeed, need only be "qualitative," the banking system being able and expected to discount the bills of all solvent persons.

But the difference between quatitative and qualitative control is not a purely financial one: It is essentially economic. Quantitative control, if it wishes to protect price stability against all danger, is necessarily restrictive. If it is unable to follow the amount of desired cash balances with sufficient accuracy, it will tend toward austerity rather than toward expansion. On the contrary, qualitative control allows the acceptance of all bills whose repayment is assured. It therefore opens wide the door to economic expansion and full employment.

Anyone who really wishes to free the economy of monetary restraints should desire, at the present time, to see quantitative control replaced by qualitative control, and therefore the return, as soon as possible, to a true money.

7

ELEMENTS FOR A
THEORY OF THE
DISCOUNT RATE AND
THE BALANCE
OF PAYMENTS

The living currency

In our complex societies, the currency is never the inert mass that the mechanistic theories of monetary phenomena envisage. It is the embodiment, in the form of bank notes or bank credits, of various assets: gold, foreign currencies, short-, medium-, or long-term claims, the amount of which varies constantly under influences which are of a monetary nature only to a very limited extent.

In particular, all the money issued as a counterpart for claims is related to the existence of such claims. When these come to maturity, the money created as a result of their being discounted at the banks is returned to the Bank of Issue, and therefore eliminated by the latter.

Thus, any volume of money generated wholly or partly by discount operations is an ever-renewed whole. If the

Extracts from an article published in *Revue Economique*, No. 4, July 1957 (Librairie Armand Colin).

amount of renewals was less than the amount of reimbursements, the volume of money would soon be exhausted.

Now, there is no direct relation between reimbursements and discount renewals. The influences that contribute to the renewal of the volume of money are numerous and dispersed. They include in particular the discount needs of private individuals, institutions and the State, bill-brokers' transactions, open-market operations, banking regulations, and the whole mass of exchange transactions.

It is an axiom of contemporary economics, however, to attribute to the "monetary authorities" a dominant influence in the determination of the quantity of money in circulation. Some writers even go so far as to contend that they completely control the volume of money.[1]

This ascription entails fundamental consequences, from the point of view of both economic theory[2] and monetary policy. It is this ascription that I wish to examine in the first instance.

Some lessons of experience concerning the so-called power of the monetary authorities

As a member of the General Council of the Bank of France, and subsequently as Assistant Governor, I have often seen the Bank of Issue worry about variations in the amount in circulation and attempt to counteract them. I have noted that these responded to its desire only to a weak extent. At no time did I have the feeling that the Bank of Issue was "changing" the quantity of money.

[1] Cf. Lord Keynes: "If we are to control the activity of the economic system by changing the quantity of money . . ." ("The General Theory of Employment, Interest and Money," p. 172). And further on: "The quantity of money is not determined by the public. All that the propensity of the public toward hoarding can achieve is to determine the rate of interest at which the aggregate desire to hoard becomes equal to the available cash." (*ibid.*, p. 174)

[2] By making it possible to imagine a situation wherein a change in the "liquidity preference" would not generate any change in the quantity of money in circulation.

Even open-market operations have only a very indirect influence. Except in cases in which the variations that they tend to prompt would have occurred spontaneously—like interventions only tending to forestall seasonal variations in money circulation—the intentions of operators are nearly always thwarted by unforeseen offsetting factors.

Similarly, direct controls, the setting of floors on the amount of Treasury bills that the banks can subscribe, or on the amount of credit that they can grant, influence the quantity of money only to the very variable extent that they do not bring about inverse reactions in the other currency-generating processes. In any case, they do not determine directly the amount issued.

As Director of the French Treasury (Mouvement général des Fonds), from 1936 to 1939, I had the feeling that the situation of the Treasury had a profound influence on the quantity of money in circulation. However, that influence was indirect and could never be foreseen. Every Thursday, the Bank of France notified me of the balance of the Treasury account. The balance was the result of countless transactions that had been carried out all over the national territory and were known only *ex post facto*. The objective items—the deficit of the Treasury, liquidity requirements—had only a minor influence on the issue of currency compared with the factors of psychological origin, such as the amount of Treasury bills subscribed or movements in total savings banks deposits. I have known periods of galloping inflation as well as stability, or even deflation, to exist within an identical technical context.

It did not appear to me that the Treasury controlled the quantity of money in circulation any more than did the monetary authorities.

I am not contending that the monetary or revenue authorities do not influence the volume of money—nothing would farther from the truth; I only claim that they do not determine the amount and are often unable to change it as they please.[1]

[1] See Post script, Chapter VII.

The sovereignty of
the money users

Any attempt to identify the influences that determine the quantity of money in circulation is conditioned by one essential fact, namely that the users of cash balances are free to determine as they please the amount of such balances. To my knowledge, it has never occurred that any one of them has been prevented from increasing or reducing his cash balance when, for any reason whatever, he wished or had to do so.

Now, the aggregate amount of money in circulation is only the sum total of the cash balances that money users keep in their note cases or in their tills.

The fact—which is indisputable—that they always come by the quantity of money they need or desire, proves with certainty that in determining the amount of their cash balances, they influence the sources of supply of such balances.

While each one of us is, within the amount of his assets, the absolute master of the level of his cash balance, it is by purchasing less or selling more that he can increase it, and by buying more and selling less that he can reduce it.

Accordingly, it is through his demand or supply interventions in the market that each of us can influence the quantity of money available to satisfy his needs.

Any monetary theory desirous of accounting for the facts must in the first instance throw light on the mechanism through which this influence is felt.

The joint effects of an increase
in supply or a diminution of
demand in the market

Additional supplies or diminutions of demand can relate to real wealth or to claims. When they occur in an economy that is operating normally, they bring about a decline in prices in the former case, and an increase in the rates on the market in the latter.[1]

To gain an insight into the relations between these two movements, let us assume for a moment that the additional supplies or the diminutions of demand relate to an assortment of items having the same composition as the whole range of goods traded in the market. Such an assortment would include real wealth and claims in a definite ratio.

On this assumption, any additional supplies and any restriction of demand would bring about price declines and rate increases simultaneously and in equally defined proportions. The two movements would thus be indissolubly connected in the market.

In reality, the excess of supplies and the restrictions of demand will in the first instance concern special assets, i.e., real wealth or claims, the nature of which cannot be foreseen and will depend on the assets held by the economic agent who wishes to increase his cash balance. Most often, in fact, they will concern short-term claims and will affect the money market directly.

But I have explained elsewhere[2] that the two movements,

[1] It goes without saying that additional supplies or a diminution of demand affect in the first instance the price of the wealth to which they relate.

But any specific price shift in the price scale tends to produce shifts in production capabilities. Such shifts tend to spread the effect of the initial disturbance over the whole of the price scale.

Induction effects of this type tend to maintain a certain degree of permanence in the price hierarchy. Naturally, there will in fact be distortions, which vary depending on the location of the initial disturbance and whose magnitude and duration will be in an inverse ratio to price sensitivity in the market under consideration.

If certain prices are pegged by the authorities, the effects of the initial disturbance will be concentrated on those prices that remain free in the market.

If there are no free prices, the disturbance produces the effects characteristic of "repressed inflation."

Stricter theorizing would involve the use of the "point of production" concept as outlined in *L'Ordre social*, 2nd ed., p. 52 (Librairie de Médicis, 1949).

[2] Cf. above, "Influences Regulating the Amount of Currency and the Institutional Problem of Money," Chapter VI; and *L'ordre social*, p. 211.

i.e., the movement of prices and the movement of interest rates, were indissolubly linked and that if one occurred separately, it tended to generate the other.

In order to keep this exposé within reasonable bounds, I shall present in a footnote[1] the mechanism responsible for this relation. I know that several of my colleagues question its existence. I would ask them to give some thought to the considerations that, to me, demonstrate its existence, because I fail to perceive—in the light of the considerations expounded in Section V, c, below—how the supply of the

[1] The contention is that if one of the movements—the interest rate movement or the price movement—occurs in isolation, it will draw the other after it.

The rise in the short-term interest rate, for instance, should it occur without any change having taken place in the demand for real wealth, will make it a paying proposition to sell for cash and buy back on a forward basis, and to invest in the money market the funds derived from the sale until the repurchase is settled, thereby bringing about a decline in spot prices.

Inversely, the decline in spot prices, should it occur without any change having taken place in the demand for short-term bills, will make it a paying proposition to buy for cash and sell on a forward basis, and to discount in the money market the bills derived from the sale for the settlement of the purchase, thereby bringing about an increase in the rate in the money market.

If, under the existing system, there were not enough short-term bills to provide, through discounts, the additional desired cash balances, forward prices would rise, relatively to spot prices. This would deflect supplies from spot markets to forward markets. This would generate the additional bills required for providing the additional desired cash balances.

Thus, in all cases, desire for additional cash balances will tend to lower prices and raise the short-term rate.

The coexistence, in periods of nonrepressed inflation, of high rates and increasing prices is urged against this reasoning. It is true that any substantial deficit tends to generate a marked excess of supply over demand for Treasury bills. Such an excess tends to push the money market rates to very high levels. It is precisely the fact that this increase in interest rates is brought under control and checked, the moment the market rate has hit the level of the discount rate, that brings about inflation. When the discount rate is raised, the market rate is drawn after it so long as the former remains below the level at which the latter would have established itself spontaneously. Thus, in such circumstances the rate of the money market may appear high compared to what it had been before the deficit occurred, but it remains always lower and, in general, considerably lower, than the level at which it would have to be if the market was to be in balance without any discount.

desired cash balances could be effectively ensured if such relation did not exist.

Furthermore, the standard-assortment assumption—a supply and demand unit incorporating all the items traded in the market—leads to a clear and direct perception of the existence of a relation between a fall in prices and a rise in interest rates. This alone constitutes a strong presumption in favor of the relation expounded in the foregoing footnote.

Solidarity between the price effect and the rate effect is secured by an induction mechanism similar to that which confers a certain permanence on the price hierarchy. As a result, distortions will occur that will vary depending on the nature of the initial impulse and the degree of sensitivity of the various markets. They may result, in particular, in marked differences between the short-term claims market—commonly referred to as the money market—and the long-term claims market, or financial market.

It goes without saying that a thorough econometrical study should submit my analysis to factual controls. I have only been able to collect, in Section VI below, some presumptive evidence of an experimental nature. I hope that econometrists will agree to explore the problem of the links between the spot and forward phenomena, therefore between the rate and the prices, which in any case is a prerequisite to any analysis of monetary mechanisms.

Supplying cash balances in the various monetary systems

Nothing is more contingent than monetary systems. Money in our complex societies is a purely institutional creation, the modalities of which may vary infinitely.

What makes up a currency is its widespread acceptance in trade. In its extreme forms, a currency unit may be a mere token devoid of any intrinsic value—such as a piece of paper imprinted with the stamp of a privileged issuer—or a real wealth endowed, as a result of its very nature, with a certain trading power and assuming the nature of money as a result of the tacit consent of all trading partners in the market.

In the first case, the quantity of money in circulation can be increased at the will of the authorities that print it or reduced by them in proportion to their availabilities. It is maintained at an immutable level if the issuing authority decides neither to create nor to eliminate any amount.

In the latter case, on the contrary, money comes and goes at the will of its users. Its quantity is that of the monetary wealth that economic agents are disposed to use as currency.

Currencies of the first type are completely inelastic. Those of the second type, on the contrary, would be fully elastic if economic impulses were transmitted forthwith.

Existing monetary systems are variously situated between these two extremes.

SUPPLYING CASH BALANCES IN
TOTALLY INELASTIC MONETARY
SYSTEMS

Let us assume, to be specific, that the currency is made up exclusively of bank notes which have no counterpart whatsoever, but are printed by an issuing authority enjoying a legal privilege, in strictly constant quantities. Let us assume further that the creation and destruction of money are both liable to severe penalties.

Let us imagine that within such a system, the money-users wish, for instance as the period of holidays draws near, to increase their cash balances.

In order to bring into relief the effects of the decision they make, one must proceed on the basis of an economy operating normally.

The meaning of this assumption is fully brought out if one considers that any economy is a community of economic agents, producers, tradesmen, civil servants, who exercise demand and supply in the market.

A retailer, for instance, will be operating normally if he

buys fruit and vegetables in the morning and sells them before the end of the day in order to be able, with the cash balance thus reconstituted, to renew indefinitely the economic cycle characteristic of his trade.

A civil servant will be operating normally if in the course of the month he spends on consumer goods or for investment purposes the salary cashed at the beginning of the month and is thus able, here again, to renew indefinitely the interventions in the market that his behavior involves.

Each individual cycle requires at any moment the existence of a certain cash balance without which the cycle could not be completed.

Thus, if he buys on a spot basis, the retailer mentioned above must have every morning a cash balance equal to the value of his purchases. As a result of his purchases, that cash balance will flow into the assets of various producers and will revert to him as and when he sells the goods.

Similarly, a civil servant will, at the beginning of the month, have a cash balance equal to the amount of his salary. He will spend this cash balance during the month and have the same amount again at the beginning of the next month.

It goes without saying that any change in the rate of settlements or the temporary reimbursement of bank debts would affect the amount of cash balances related to a certain production-consumption cycle. But within a given situation of monetary habits, the amount of the cash balance specifically related to each individual cycle is at every moment precisely determined and strictly essential for the financing of that cycle.

We regard it as the *necessary cash balance* of the economic agent under consideration.

So long as payments habits do not change, the amount of the necessary cash balance depends only on the volume, expressed in kind, of the transactions that are characteristic of the cycle and on the price at which they are effected.

All other conditions being equal as regards the volume in kind of the transactions effected, it depends solely on prices.

However, no economic agent limits the amount of the cash balance that he holds to the amount of his "necessary cash balance." In order to be able to meet any possible needs, he retains additional amounts of money that are determined by purely psychological considerations and constitutes his *hoarded cash balance.*

The sum of the necessary cash balance and the hoarded cash balance we consider to be the *desired cash balance* of the economic agent under consideration.[1]

The above analysis makes it possible to forecast the consequences, within a fully inelastic monetary system, of an increase in the desired cash balance brought about by an increase—for instance at the end of the month or on the eve of the holiday period—in the amount of hoarded cash balances with a view to the settlements expected.[2]

The increase in supply or the diminution of demand, intended to provide the additional desired cash balances, bring about a price decline in the normally operating economy that we are considering here. The price diminution reduces the amount of the cash balances necessary for the settlement of transactions. The diminution of the necessary cash balances releases, and thereby provides, the additional desired cash balances, without any change occurring in the quantity of money in circulation.

[1] The concepts of "necessary cash balance" and "hoarded cash balance" are substituted for the concept of "velocity of circulation" of money and make this last one unnecessary. One could say, however, that the velocity of circulation of the necessary cash balance is objectively defined by the characteristics of the economic cycle the financing of which it ensures, while the velocity of circulation of the hoarded cash balance is zero. (See on this point *L'ordre social,* Chapter XIV, concerning "Encaisse nécessaire et encaisse désirée." ("Necessary Cash Balance and Desired Cash Balance.") After having abundantly used the concept of velocity of circulation and even having attempted to measure it in my *Théorie des phénomènes monétaires,* Chapter IV, pp. 135 *et seq.* (Payot, 1927), I have given up the idea of using it because it has appeared to me as being a purely mathematical expression, devoid of any psychological or human reality. None of us knows how or ever proposes to modify the velocity of circulation of his money. On the contrary, the necessary cash balance is an economic reality that is clearly defined by reference to monetary habits, and the hoarded cash balance is a psychological reality, the amount of which can be known exactly at any moment.

[2] An increase in the desired cash balance resulting from an augmentation in the necessary cash balance subsequent upon a rise in the volume of employment would have the same effects.

A diminution of the hoarded cash balances would, *mutatis mutandis,* have inverse effects.

Thus, in an inelastic monetary system, any variation in the desired cash balance would be followed by an inverse variation of the general price level. Things would take place as if that part of circulation that was allocated to the provision of the necessary cash balances was the only reserve that could be tapped to provide the additional desired cash balances or that could be used to reabsorb the undesired elements of cash.

Now, in fact the aggregate amount of the desired cash balances varies constantly, not only for psychological reasons which influence the hoarded cash balances, but also depending on variations in the necessary cash balances resulting from the monthly or seasonal rate of transactions and on variations in the degree of economic activity, more particularly the expansion of production.

Any lack of expansion or contraction capacity in the quantity of money depending on requirements would generate constant instability in the general price level.

It is in order to guard against such instability that all modern States have adopted monetary systems enabling the quantity of money in circulation to be adjusted to the aggregate amount of desired cash balances.

SUPPLYING CASH BALANCES IN
EXCLUSIVELY METALLIC
MONETARY SYSTEMS

Systems based only on metallic currencies afford the most straightforward example of elastic systems. They are characterized by freedom of minting at a fixed rate, and freedom of melting. Being at liberty to mint currency, the issuing authority takes up at an immutable price all the quantities of metal supplied but not demanded in the market in order to monetize them.

Where such a system exists, any increase in the desired cash balances brings about, *caeteris paribus,* a decline in the general price level. Such a decline tends to divert certain production capabilities from the production of nonmonetary wealth, the price of which has declined, to the production of gold, the only type of wealth whose price has not changed, thereby tending to increase gold production. Now, the additional amount of metal supplied but not demanded is, *caeteris paribus,* converted into currency, thereby providing—without any variation in the general level of prices—the additional cash balances desired.

I hope no one will object here that such a mechanism is purely theoretical. All the statistics show that gold production reacts to variations in the general level of prices. But they also show that production variations occur only very slowly, when the variations that tend to bring them about have reached a sufficient degree of magnitude. This lack of responsiveness on the part of gold production is much increased as a result of restrictions on gold dealings. An exclusively metallic system would therefore generate considerable instability in the general price level.

It is to counteract the lack of responsiveness of purely metallic systems that all modern States have provided for the issuing of money as opposed to another type of wealth more sensitive than gold to the influences that tend to affect its production and monetization.

SUPPLYING CASH BALANCES IN
MONETARY SYSTEMS BASED EXCLU-
SIVELY ON THE MONETIZATION OF
CLAIMS EXPRESSED IN CURRENCY;
INTRODUCTION OF THE DISCOUNT
RATE

If wealth other than gold is to be convertible into currency without any risk for the issuing institution, such wealth must, like gold under a system of metal convertibility at a fixed rate, have a fixed value in terms of money. Now, only claims expressed in money present this feature *at the time of maturing.* Therefore they alone, except in a system of convertible currency the conversion wealth, can provide the raw material for currency, provided however that the maturity date is on an average not too remote, so that the amount of daily maturities will always be in excess of the amount of cash balances that might have to be reabsorbed in any one day.

Under such a system, monetization is effected by entering a claim on the credit side of a bank ledger, against the entering on the debit side of the debt represented by either the bank notes put in circulation or, more generally, the amount credited to the account of the party selling the claim.

The purchase of the claim by the bank is effected at a certain price that represents the current value of the paper sold and determines the rate at which such paper has been discounted by the bank.

In fact, the modalities of monetization are made more intricate by provisions conferring on one or more banks a monopoly over the issue of legal tender. In order to avoid such complications, I shall assume that there is only one bank in the community considered and that all the currency issued by this institution in the form of bank notes or bank credits is in the nature of legal tender. The bank, whether acting under mandatory regulations or legal provisions, or by virtue of a decision freely arrived at by its own authorities, is constantly taking up, at the rate it chooses to determine—and such rate we shall call the *discount rate*—the bills presented to it amongst those that meet its "discount eligibility" standards.[1]

Let us examine the effects, in such a system, of an increase in hoarded cash balances caused, for instance, by the approach of the holiday period.

Any individual who, within the framework of an activity that is operating normally, wishes to increase his cash balances must either supply more or demand less.

The resulting increase in supply or diminution of de-

[1] Other monetization procedures, in particular open-market operations, are examined in Section VI below.

mand—whether they directly affect the standard assortment reflecting the composition of market exchanges or, whether as a result of the induction effects referred to in the footnote on the same page, everything happens as if this were the case —generate simultaneously and in a definite ratio a supply of real wealth and of claims which is not matched by demand.

The supply of real wealth without a demand for it causes a decline in the general level of prices. Through the resulting diminution in the necessary cash balances, it releases quantities of money that provide the additional desired cash balances.

But at the same time, claims are being supplied and not demanded in the market where short-term claims eligible for discount are traded. We are assuming here that such a market does exist. I shall consider below the circumstances in which it can cease to exist.

In this market—which is the market outside the banks— the rate is of course lower than the discount rate since no bills would be supplied there if they could be sold in the banks at a lower rate, that is, at a higher price.

The excess of supplies of demands for claims tends to depress the prices and therefore to push up the rate that expresses such prices in the money market.

This rise in the rates, like the decline in prices, is a gradual one and at each market session depends only on the difference between supply and demand for claims to be traded against money.

It is therefore obvious that the price decline and the rate increase are one and the same phenomenon that basically expresses the price decline resulting from an excess of supplies in the market.

The price decline, whether it affects wealth proper or claims, releases the quantities of money required by the increase in hoarded cash balances, through a variation in the necessary cash balances, without any variation in the quantity of money in circulation.

But the price decline and the rate increase continue so

long as the cause that gave rise to them has not disappeared, i.e., so long as the diminution in the necessary cash balances resulting from the price decline is less than the increase in the hoarded cash balances.

The rise in the rate has the effect of bringing the monetary market rate closer to the discount rate.

If the latter is not too high, there necessarily comes a time when the former catches up with it, in other words, when the market rate hits the level of the discount rate.

From then on, all claims eligible for discount which are supplied but not demanded in the market are taken up in the banks in exchange for newly created money. The corresponding supply ceases therefore to depress the market. The rise in the rates and the decline in prices come to an end. The additional cash balances still desired are provided, not through a contraction in the necessary cash balances, but through the creation of money resulting from discount.[1]

The mechanism through which the desires of the money users govern monetary issue in a system supplied by the discount of claims thus becomes evident.

[1] This would be the place for a thorough analysis of the difference between the economic nature and consequences of the sale of an asset outside the banks in exchange for existing money, and inside the banks against newly issued money. I have attempted such an analysis in "Influences Regulating the Amount of Currency and the Institutional Problem of Money" (Chapter VI); in my opinion, it is essential for an understanding of monetary phenomena. However, several friends have told me that they had difficulty in following the reasoning. That is why I do not reproduce it here, although this will impair the rigor of the demonstration. I shall simply observe that discount outside the bank is discount effected either against the sale, during the same market session, of real wealth or other claims, therefore without any disruption of equilibrium between aggregate demand and aggregate supply during the session under consideration, or against a reduction in the desired cash balance, with the consequences resulting, for aggregate demand, from the reduction of the desired cash balances. On the other hand, discount in the banks is effected through the sale outside the market of the bill offered, therefore as against the creation of money. Such creation of money generates a corresponding increase in aggregate demand unless the quantity of newly created money is "desired" because of an increase in the necessary cash balances or the hoarded cash balances.

One should also mention specifically, while referring to the quantitative links between bank money and legal tender, the requirements that restrict the issuing capacity of a given banking system.

SUPPLYING CASH BALANCES IN
MONETARY SYSTEMS BASED EXCLUSIVELY
ON THE MONETIZATION OF FOREIGN CURRENCIES
AT FIXED RATES (GOLD-EXCHANGE STANDARD)

As in the foregoing cases, any cash balance shortage brings about an increase in the supply of or a decline in the demand for real wealth and claims.

If all other conditions are equal as regards the volume of offers (as regards employment), the resulting disequilibrium generates a decline in the price scale which stimulates exports and discourages imports. It thereby tends to generate a surplus in the balance of payments and consequently in supplies of foreign currency to be exchanged for the national currency.

Now, the bank takes up at a fixed rate, in exchange for money which it creates, the foreign currency supplied for which there is no demand. As this movement continues and gains momentum so long as the generating factor does not disappear, it cannot furnish the additional desired cash balances.

A balance-of-payments deficit arising from nonmonetary causes would have the same effect, whereas a surplus in the actual cash balances or in the balance of payments would have inverse effects.

I am fully aware that there will be some jeering about the unreal nature of this analysis and that it will be criticized having regard to the volume of international trade, which on account of its particular nature is not subject to the influence of price differentials. There is no doubt that a substantial part of international transactions is determined by noneconomic —i.e., political, military, and even charitable—considerations. But once they have been carried out, they, together with all commercial transactions, leave a balance which has to be settled.

It is the balance thus generated, whatever its nature or amount, that inevitably brings into play the adjustment mechanism outlined above.

Moreover, experience confirms that notwithstanding the

rigidity of certain balance-of-payments items, an important part of international transactions in all Western countries in fact remains sensitive to price disparities.

Furthermore, the monetization of foreign exchange is, after all, only one of the sources of money. The analysis in Section VIII below will demonstrate how, if the balance of payments showed little elasticity, the other sources of money would take the place of the foreign currency monetization factor.

Confrontation with reality

Some practical operators will contend that the above analysis is far removed from the facts. They will not recognize facts with which they are familiar, on the assumption of a market where short-term bills or foreign currencies are traded while banks look on indifferently and merely consent to "take up" certain assets supplied but not demanded which brokers, eager to reap differences, present to them.

Here I shall give special consideration to the money market.

It is a fact that for several decades Banks of Issue have been playing, within the framework of their open-market policies, an active rather than a passive role in the monetary market, taking the initiative of buying and selling bills of varying maturities in the market at rates lower than the discount rate, without being requested to do so.

Such interventions alter the form but not the substance of monetary processes. In the case of a Bank of Issue, the purchase of bills which differ from those that under its statutes it regards as eligible for discount merely amounts to making such bills temporarily eligible for discount during the period of purchase. To buy bills normally eligible for discount at a rate lower than the discount rate is only equivalent to bringing the discount rate down to the level corresponding to the price at which the transaction takes place, during the period of purchase.

The Federal Reserve System pushed this procedure to an extreme by assuming the task, over a prolonged period which, I believe, ended in 1952, of stabilizing Federal funds rates through purchases effected as against the creation of money. Such a policy had no other effect than to make such funds whose prices had been stabilized eligible for discount at a rate corresponding to the purchase price.

Bank of Issue technicians are also of opinion that the regulations imposed on private banks hamper the functioning of the market as described above—in particular in France, as a result of the decisions taken by the Council of Credit (Conseil du Crédit), and in the United States through the varying regulations concerning the reserve ratios.

There is no doubt that the regulation of banking activities affects banking behavior and may force banks to make purchases or sales that they would not otherwise effect if they were prompted only by rates considerations. Thus, such regulations influence demands for cash balances or claims, but not the procedure through which such demands are met.

One can easily conceive of a situation wherein the Bank of Issue, forestalling market supplies or market demands, would maintain full stability of its rates through market operations, thereby making it unnecessary for the market to come to the bank. The Bank of England was formerly believed to be anxious to bring about such a situation to the greatest extent possible. The Federal Reserve System was also creating a similar situation in the Federal funds market at the time when it pegged their rates.

The active interventions of the banks, in particular through their open-market operations, together with existing regulations combine to form the market situation and to determine the market rates, in particular as regards bills eligible for discount.

All such interventions influence the quantity of money in circulation. But the essential point is that if, at any time, the quantity of money in circulation is less than the aggregate amount of the desired cash balances, the mechanism described previously comes into play. The general level of prices, whatever it may be at that particular point in time, will tend to fall and the market rates will tend to rise. The moment the rates for bills eligible for discount reach the level of the discount rate, that part of such bills which is supplied but for which there is no demand will, as a result of the automatic intervention of brokers, be taken to the banks to be monetized.

It may happen that distortions in the scale of prices or rates resulting from interventions by the authorities, or delays in transmission which vary depending on the point where the initial impulse occurred, affect the unfolding of the process. But the cause that tends to bring about these phenomena, i.e., the difference between the aggregate amount of the desired cash balances and actual circulation, will make its influence felt until such time as these phenomena have produced their effect.

All the observations that it has been given me to make and all the evidence that I have collected bear out this conclusion. I shall only quote one example, derived from the experience of the United States.

No system is more complicated, more closely regulated, more remote from automaticity, in a word more "active" than the Federal Reserve System.

Now, in a booklet published by the Federal Reserve Bank of New York in 1952 (Money Market Essays), the foregoing analysis has been confirmed beyond dispute.

First, the mechanism through which the market rates are adjusted is analyzed:

> During the early postwar years member bank borrowing from the Federal Reserve System was for the most part a tool by which large money market and correspondent banks could keep their cash reserves at a minimum and their earning assets at a maximum. Toward the end of 1951, however, as the Reserve Banks, in their open market operations, began to show an increasing reluctance to supply the market with reserves to carry it over periods of temporary stringency, the resort to borrowing became much more widespread.
>
> Banks regularly assess their future needs for funds, and

attempt to manage their loan and investment portfolios so as to be able to meet those needs as they arise. But most banks, and particularly those in money market centers, encounter periods of temporary money market tightness when they lose reserves unexpectedly through a withdrawal of funds from the market in connection with unforeseen security transactions, gold outflows, or other factors. Since large banks find it profitable to keep their resources as fully invested as possible and therefore seldom maintain substantial excess reserves for more than a few days at most, such losses of funds are likely to draw their reserves down below the required level. Banks may obtain funds to tide them over such periods in one of three ways: (1) sell securities; (2) buy reserves ("Federal funds") from other banks which have excess reserves; or (3) borrow from a Reserve Bank. (A bank could also call loans, but this is not likely procedure today, particularly for the short run.) The choice of method depends primarily on two factors—the cost and the length of time the funds will be needed. If a bank expects its money position to ease shortly, as a result of such factors as an inflow of funds from correspondent banks or a return flow of currency, it is likely first to try to buy (borrow) Federal funds. If they are not available in adequate volume at a satisfactory price, it will borrow or sell securities, depending upon cost. (If the market is tight, the sale of even short-term securities may be relatively costly.) If a reserve deficiency is expected to be of some duration, the bank will probably sell securities, although it may have to borrow until it finds an acceptable bid for its securities.

Smaller banks have generally not made as much use of the borrowing privilege. They usually try to keep their deposits at the Reserve Banks above the required level, since the expense of keeping a constant watch on their reserve positions and of making continual adjustments in their assets is likely to be greater than the additional income which they could realize by keeping fully invested. However, some of the smaller banks, particularly those in agricultural or resort areas, have strong seasonal swings in both deposits and demands for loans. These banks often borrow from the Reserve Banks prior to their lending season in order to be able to meet their customers' demands for working capital, and they repay their borrowings after crops are marketed or the vacation season draws to a close. Although many more banks have borrowed for seasonal purposes in recent years than have borrowed for day-to-day reserve adjustment purposes, seasonal loans have accounted for only a small proportion of the dollar volume of total member bank borrowing.

But the most decisive confirmation comes from a chart in the booklet on page 14:

FEDERAL FUNDS RATE IN NEW YORK CITY
(Daily for the Fourth Quarter of 1951*)

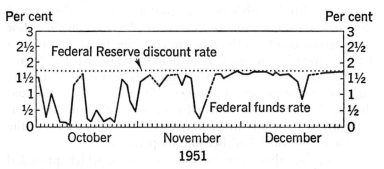

* The figures shown represent the modal rate for each week day's trans-actions; holidays are indicated by dashed lines.
    SOURCE: Garvin, Bantel & Company.

This chart shows that until recent years no amount of stabilizing interventions on the part of the Federal System prevented pulsations in the market rates or stopped them from hitting the level of the discount rate when, after all stabilizing interventions had been made, the market still demanded additional cash balances. The chart shows that the discount rate of the Federal Reserve Bank of New York came very close to the rate at which Federal funds were traded, the latter being available balances of the Federal Reserve Banks, that is, funds on demand.

The London and Paris markets would, *mutatis mutandis,* provide the same teaching, as is evidenced by the following extract from the market bulletin in the *Economist* of May 26, 1956:

> Credit in Lombard Street has remained short this week. Before the week-end the Bank made small special purchases, and on Tuesday after the (Whitsun) holiday three or four houses were obliged to take a very small amount at Bank rate, despite some small further special purchases.

Thus, by "going to the market," the bank does not always succeed in preventing the market from "coming to it"—and when it does, it is the mechanism of the rates that ensures the final adjustment of the quantity of money effectively issued to the aggregate amount of the desired cash balances.

Before I finish with this confrontation of the theory and the facts, I would wish to answer an objection made a few years ago by two English colleagues of mine to whose opinion I attach great importance. They held the view that the "structural" changes that had occurred since the war had completely eliminated the monetary markets. They held the view that the supplying of money was effected only by voluntary interventions by the bank, through open-market operations, as the mechanism of rates had become inoperative.

It is a fact that open-market operations, which provided the market at any moment with the quantity of money that the market itself would have demanded from the bank, through discount operations, if the issuing authorities had abstained from intervening, would eliminate any movement in the rates and any recourse to discount with a bank. But this would be a substitution effect within unchanged structures, rather than a structural modification. The above quotations and the chart show further that this result has never been fully attained. Now, so long as it is not attained, the residual need for cash balances is met through the mechanism of the rates previously described.

It may happen, however, that over a prolonged period, if not permanently, the discount rate is fixed at a level lower than the rate which would bring about a balance between supplies of and demands for money in exchange for bills eligible for discount in the monetary market. This is what happens in particular when the public finance deficit induces the Treasury to supply such large quantities of Treasury bills that the market in which they are offered could find its balance only at an extremely high rate, out of all proportion to the usual rates. In such a case, the rate for the bills offered is fixed at or sufficiently close to the level of the discount rate so that subscribers are induced to buy the bills offered and to present them for discount with the banks after a short period.

Where such a situation exists—and it has existed in varying forms in all inflationary periods—there is practically no longer any market, because if a market is to exist, there must be a supply and a demand. But the moment the supply of bills declines, a market re-emerges, shyly, at first in the middle of the month, when availabilities are fairly plentiful, and is subsequently re-established on a continuing basis. Any change due to exceptional and temporary circumstances cannot be regarded as being of a structural nature.

The manifestations of the monetary phenomena are complicated by the existence of legal tender which the central bank alone issues. The issuing monopoly thus established forces the banks issuing credit money to maintain part of their assets in real money, or in the form of deposits with the central bank.

The need to maintain such assets at an appropriate level affects the demand for money in the market, but does not substantially alter the mechanism described above through which the money is provided.

Nature of the discount rate

The stability of the general level of prices can be jeopardized by an excess of aggregate demand over the aggregate value of supplies or by an excess of the aggregate amount of desired cash balances over the total quantity of money in circulation.

The disturbance can therefore arise on either the demand side or the money side. But it is essential never to forget that any scarcity of total demand relative to the aggregate value of supplies implies a demand for an additional quantity of currency,[1] and that inversely any shortage of money relative to the aggregate amount of the desired cash balances implies a shortage of total demand relative to the aggregate value of supplies.[2]

One is therefore not justified in opposing, as is too often done, the purchase-power effect and the money effect; the two are indissolubly linked by some kind of fundamental complementarity, like the two sides of an object that in this case is the disturbance considered.

In order to have a practical idea, let us consider a situation where the effective cash balance is inadequate, thereby generating in the market a supply that is not matched by a demand.

This supply without a demand will tend to reduce prices in a certain sector of the market.

I have already shown that individual price movements tended to generate movements in the whole scale of prices, with varying lags depending upon the location of the initial disturbance and the physical structures of the economy concerned.

In the case under consideration, the reduction will result from the fact that a certain part of the wealth produced is not demanded in the form in which it is offered in the market, whereas the wealth in the form of money, which is demanded, is not produced.

All regulatory monetary systems tend to offset this price shifting factor by a procedure which, at a certain level in the price scale, withdraws from the market the equivalent of the nonmonetary wealth which is supplied but not demanded,

---

[1] The reason is that the suppliers who do not demand nonmonetary wealth, i.e., real wealth or claims, in an amount not exceeding the value of their supplies during the market session when they were expressed can only demand money. If they did not demand anything, the reason would be that they were proposing to supply, but had not actually formulated a supply in the market.

[2] The reason is that those economic agents who wish to increase their cash balances must, to that effect, supply without demanding nonmonetary wealth, i.e., real wealth or claims.

and reintroduces it in the form of money, in which form it is demanded and not supplied.

Metallic convertibility, for instance, by compelling the Bank of Issue to buy (or to sell) at a certain price all the quantities of gold supplied and not demanded, maintains the price of gold, and the price of gold alone, at a constant level.[1] This privileged situation of gold tends in periods of falling prices to generate transfers of production capabilities from the production of nonmonetary wealth to that of gold, thereby tending to reduce production and therefore supply of the former, and to increase production and therefore supply of the latter. But the Bank of Issue takes up all the quantities of gold supplied but not demanded and mints them. In the process, it deflects from the market that part of production which is supplied but is not demanded, and reintroduces it in a form in which it is demanded but not supplied.

Thus, the convertibility of gold at a fixed rate creates at the level of metallic parity a *threshold* through which a part of the aggregate supply, equivalent to the excess of supply which has generated the decline, flows out of the market into the reserves of the Bank of Issue, where it is used for the minting of the additional amounts of currency demanded.

In this way, gold convertibility simply eliminates the cause that tended to generate the fall in prices.

I have shown, however, that this mechanism operated only when the initial disturbance had brought about those production shifts on which it is based. It is therefore in general not very sensitive. And in order to guard against the slowness of its functioning a similar mechanism that is much more sensitive has been established, in respect of certain types of claims, generally of a short-term nature.

When, as a result of an excess of aggregate supply over aggregate demand or a shortage of actual cash balance, the rate at which such claims are traded reaches the level of the discount rate, these flow out of the market into the assets of the banking system, which converts them into money. Such

---

1 Free minting and free melting down would, *mutatis mutandis,* have the same effect.

deflection, by reducing the aggregate supply expressed in the market by the equivalent, in value, of wealth for which there is no demand and reintroducing it in the form of money which is demanded, puts an end to the rise in rates and the decline in the general level of prices.

The discount rate too can therefore be regarded as a *threshold* providing access to the bank reserves in which the equivalent of the wealth supplied but not demanded in the market is provisionally "parked" against a receipt expressed in money. It is this feature of the discount rate that, the moment the market rate has been reached, puts an end to the excess of supply and the paucity of the cash balance that have generated the variation in the general level of prices in the market.[1]

It goes without saying that it may take a varying time before the initial disturbance affects the rate of the monetary market. In general, however, monetary needs affect banking reserves in the first instance and will be felt immediately in the monetary market. If at that time the discount rate is at the same level as the market rate or very close to it, the additional desired cash balances will be provided nearly immediately through the monetization of the undesired supply: The general level of prices will remain substantially unchanged.

If, on the other hand, the discount rate is appreciably higher than the market rate, the general level of prices will begin to fall and the rate of the monetary market will begin

---

[1] An exhaustive study should bring out that the rate for claims does not vary in relation to the general level of prices, but to variations thereof, i.e., to the derivative of the variations in the general level of prices with respect to time. It is the variations of this derivative that the discount mechanism limits, and it is by pegging it that it tends to "slow down" variations in the general level of prices wherever it happens to be, and not to bring it down to a level corresponding to the legal par value of the currency, as convertibility into gold does. The two mechanisms may coexist; but convertibility of claims at a fixed rate that is not accompanied by convertibility of metal at a fixed price only slows down the movements in the general level of prices, with varying efficiency depending on the physical environment wherein it operates (location of the initial disturbance, greater or lesser rigidity of the economic systems). In any case, such convertibility is indifferent to the general level of prices which it brings about.

to rise. The additional desired cash balances will be provided as a result of the contraction of the amount of the necessary cash balances resulting from this twofold movement, which will continue until such time as the rate of the monetary market reaches the level of the discount rate.

From then on, but not before, the general level of prices and the rate of the monetary market will no longer vary.

Therefore, it is the situation of the discount rate in relation to the market rate which, *caeteris paribus,* determines the possible margin of instability of the general level of prices and of the level of the market rate.

The closer the discount rate is to the market rate, the more limited possible variations in the general level of prices resulting from a given disequilibrium between aggregate supply and aggregate demand or a given variation in the desired cash balances, but on the other hand the more unstable the quantity of money in circulation.

Inversely, the farther the rate of discount is from the market rate, the more stable the quantity of money in circulation in periods of variations in the desired cash balances, and the more unstable the general level of prices.[1]

Suggestions toward a theory of international trade

The foregoing analysis enables us to pose the problem of international trade in a realistic context.

Classical theories depart from such a context to the extent that they consider that a balance-of-payments deficit must of

1 The above analysis shows that if the relation between price movements and rate movements did not exist, monetary systems based on the monetization of claims could not operate. If they are to operate, it is indeed necessary for the excess of supply of real wealth that may have been generated by a demand for additional cash balances to be felt in the monetary market in order to produce there the increase in the supply of short-term bills which generates additional amounts of money. The fact that systems based on the monetization of claims do function, and function well, is in itself a proof of the existence of the relation in question.

necessity generate a contraction in aggregate purchasing power that tends to guard against the generating disequilibrium in a direct manner—that is, by influencing international trade.

I propose to show that this is the case only in certain well-defined circumstances and that the theory which contends that it is always so is wrong.

For the sake of simplification, I shall assume that gold and foreign currencies are concentrated in the assets of the banking system and can be drawn out—as is the case at present in the United States—only for settlements abroad. I shall assume further, in order not to confuse the issue, that, in the case of each market participant, his actual cash balance equates his desired cash balance.

If at a given market session the balance of international payments is in deficit, the amount of settlements to be affected abroad is in excess of the amount of the settlements expected from abroad.

The foreign exchange necessary for settlement of the unrequited balance must be obtained from the banks.

Since we have assumed that the effective cash balances equate the desired cash balances, the resources necessary for the purchase of such foreign exchange cannot be obtained from such cash balances. Demanders of foreign exchange must therefore secure it by supplying nonmonetary wealth in the market. They pay the amounts derived from such supplies into the banks, which provide them with the foreign exchange that they need. They therefore do not express any demand in the market, and the cash balances that they pay into the banks are reabsorbed.

Thus, the balance-of-payments deficit has a twofold affect during the market session at which it is settled:

a. From the point of view of aggregate market equilibrium, it gives rise to supplies up to the amount of the deficit which are not matched by corresponding demands;

b. From the point of view of money, it generates an actual cash balance shortage of the same amount.

The supply-without-demand causes a fall in prices if it

affects real wealth, and a rise in the rate if it affects claims (the rise in the rate being only a reflection of the fall in the price of claims).

If we admit, as we have in the foregoing paragraphs, that the two movements are indissolubly connected, they bring about all or some of the following consequences:

a. A diminution, as a result of the fall in prices, of the cash balances necessary for settlement of the transactions. Such diminution releases the cash balances which will bring the individual cash balances back to the desired level;

b. An increase in exports, as a result of the contraction of aggregate domestic demand or the fall of domestic prices relative to foreign prices, the latter phenomenon occurring to the extent that the former has not produced its effects directly or immediately. Now the foreign buyer, in order to settle his purchase, makes a supply in his own market. His action therefore generates a demand-without-supply which restores aggregate equilibrium in the market, whilst the settlement for his purchase brings the actual circulation back to the level of the aggregate amount of the desired cash balances, through the monetization of foreign exchange[1];

c. An increase in domestic output of gold, as a result of the fact that the fall in the scale of prices leaves one single sale price unchanged—the price at which the central bank purchases gold. Now, the sale of gold to the central bank is a sale outside the market, whereas the purchase of the services that produced the gold is made in the market. The increase in gold production therefore generates a demand-without-supply that restores aggregate equilibrium in the market, while the monetization of newly extracted gold brings actual circulation back to the aggregate level of the desired cash balances.

d. An intensification of discounting operations at the banks, the moment the market rate reaches the level of the

[1] One could also conceive of the inflow of foreign capital attracted by the rise in the rates of claims as a settlement procedure. But the resulting sale of claims is only one particular form of export. It is therefore only a part of the effect considered in the previous paragraph and does not need to be analyzed separately.

discount rate. Such intensification of discounts at the banks provides the discounter with new monetary units, created as a result of the discounting operation with the bank. Since his desired cash balance is assumed to be at the level of his actual cash balance, he will increase his demand in the market by a corresponding amount. The resulting demand-without-supply restores aggregate balance in the market, while the creation of new money brings actual circulation back to the aggregate level of the desired cash balances. This latter process results in gold or foreign exchange being replaced in the balance sheet of the banking system by short-term paper in national currency. It reduces correspondingly the percentage of cover for the currency.

In fact, it is through one of the four processes outlined above that the regulating mechanism will restore equilibrium in the balance of payments. The first three will bring about a situation of steady operating normalcy which can last indefinitely; the fourth will gradually deplete the reserves of the banking system.

Now, the switching to one or other of the four alternative channels will depend on the elasticity of prices and exports, the cost of domestic gold production, and the specific position of the discount rate relatively to the rate outside the banks.

Everything takes place as if the means necessary for the restoration of equilibrium could be drawn from four different sources: actual circulation, foreign trade, gold lying deep in the ground, gold and foreign exchange deep in the reserves of the banking system. A threshold situated at a given level commands access to each of these means. It is in fact the first threshold to be reached that provides the resources which will restore equilibrium.

If one assumes that the cost of gold is high in relation to the price at which the Banks of Issue purchase it, as is the case in most Western countries, the third alternative is ruled out. The first does not obviate the need to resort to the exchange reserves of the banking system. It is therefore solely by increasing exports or reducing imports on the one hand, and by calling on convertibility reserves on the other, that one can restore balance-of-payments equilibrium. All other conditions being equal as regards the elasticity of international exchanges, the choice between the two alternatives will depend only on the situation of the discount rate relative to the rate outside the banks at the particular point in time.

If the discount rate is far in excess of the monetary market rate, the margin for the lowering of prices is quite considerable. The likelihood of equilibrium being restored through a reduction of imports and an increase of exports is considerable.

If, on the contrary, the discount rate happens to be at the same level as the market rate, the deficit will be settled by resorting to discount and drawing on foreign exchange reserves.

The importance of the level of the discount rate thus becomes obvious. By moving it away from the rate outside the banks, one raises the threshold which commands recourse to the reserves of the Bank of Issue. The likelihood of restoring equilibrium in international trade is thereby increased.

If, where such equilibrium exists, one raises the rate of discount, one brings about the substitution of discounts in the market for discounts in the banks coming to maturity and thereby, *caeteris paribus,* and through the twofold consequence of the income- and price-effects, an increase in exports or a reduction in imports. The resulting modification in the balance of international trade increases by a corresponding amount the gold or foreign exchange reserve of the banking system.

The determination of the rate of exchange therefore provides the banking authorities with an instrument with which they can change as they please the amount of gold and foreign exchange in bank assets.

The above analysis, however, is valid only to the extent that the discount rate is above the rate of equilibrium in the monetary market. Now, the deficit, which generates a supply of bills in the market that is permanently in excess of the demand, causes the market rate to stick to the rate in the banks. It therefore provides immediate access to the reserves of the banking system with a view to restoring equilibrium in international exchanges, thereby excluding in practice any possibility of such equilibrium being restored through an increase in exports or a reduction in imports, as well as any increase in the gold or foreign exchange reserves.

Before ending this section and knowing full well that I am somewhat repetitious, I am particularly anxious, in order to avoid unnecessary polemics, to stress that I am fully aware that there are certain noneconomic elements in the balances of payments, that some of these result from governmental decisions and may even be due only to political or generous motives. But international exchanges as a whole, regardless of the motives on which they are based, will leave a balance that has to be settled, and such settlement cannot but generate in the markets that are not fully regulated by authoritative interventions the phenomena that have been outlined, considering that the influence which brings them about gains momentum until one of the results that it tends to prompt has been obtained. Furthermore, recent developments in many countries provide factual evidence in support of this analysis.

Principles of a discount policy

Contemporary monetary systems are based on the monetization of gold, of certain foreign currencies, and of claims expressed in national currency. The volume of money is therefore the product of countless influences that, to a large extent, are unrelated. Those assets which are the counterpart thereof are constantly renewed as a result of discounted claims coming to maturity.

About the volume of money generated by all such transactions we know only one thing, i.e., that in each moment it will be what it has to be if the users of money are to hold the cash balances that they desire to hold. But the way in which it will be what it has to be, in other words the process of monetization which gives rise to it and the assets which constitute its counterpart, depend essentially on the will of the monetary authorities.

Indeed, by fixing the level of the rate of discount, or of the rate at which open-market purchasing and selling trans-actions are made, relative to the level of the market rate, the monetary authorities direct the money-creating processes as between the various sources from which they can be supplied.

If the discount rate is very close to the market rate, any previous discount reimbursement generates a paucity in the actual cash balances and through the rate tightness that it causes drives to the banks the renewal bills supplied in the market.

If, on the other hand, the discount rate is appreciably in excess of the market rate, the latter can rise over a prolonged period without such rise causing any creation of money. The substitution money will be provided either through a reduc-tion in the necessary cash balances resulting from the fall in prices, or through the monetization operations resulting from foreign payments due to the improvement in the balance of payments subsequent upon the fall of prices or the rise in the rates.

While the situation of the discount rate or of the rate at which open-market transactions are effected relative to the market rate determines the switching of renewal discounts in conditions of steady operating normalcy, it determines in the same way the channels through which the demands sub-sequent upon any disturbance in the previously existing equilibrium will be met, whether such disturbance results from a change in the balance-of-payments situation or a varia-tion in the aggregate level of the desired cash balances.

It goes without saying that the generality of such results leaves a certain margin of uncertainty which is a function, in particular because of the fact that the various economic re-sponses are not equally sensitive, of the location of the initial disturbance.

With this reservation, one can say that by fixing the situation of the discount rate relative to the market rate, the monetary authorities determine the composition of the assets which constitute the counterpart of the monetary issue, and the nature of the effects generated—in particular as regards the general level of prices—by any disturbance occurring in the market. The maintenance of the rate of discount at the level of the market rate will generate stability in the general level of prices and instability in the quantity of money in circulation. Inversely, the maintenance of the rate of discount at a level appreciably in excess of the market rate will generate instability in the general level of prices and stability in the quantity of money in circulation.

The control of the rate at which open-market transactions are effected is therefore an extremely powerful instrument in the hands of the monetary authorities.

However, a fundamental reservation is necessary. If the discount rate is to enable the monetary authorities to orientate the demands for money in the market, they must be in a position to fix it, as they wish, at the same level as the market rate or above.

Now, there are circumstances wherein the rate that would secure equilibrium in the monetary market would be so high that no monetary authority would in fact agree to set the discount rate at the same or at a higher level. Such is the case in particular when the supply of claims eligible for discount is appreciably in excess of the market demand. In such case, the rate of discount is appreciably lower than the rate that would secure market equilibrium. So long as such a situation obtains, the actual market rate in all probability sticks to the rate of discount.

Where such a situation obtains, the needs of the market are met, as regards all that part of the supply of bills which at the discount rate is in excess of the demand, through discounting at the banks. There is no longer a monetary policy; market conditions can be altered only by action on those causes which generate the supply of bills, i.e., action of a fiscal nature or action on incomes.

Thus, the rate of discount is effective so long as it can actually be set above the market rate. The moment the discount rate is appreciably lower than the rate at which the market would be in balance, the monetary authorities are practically divested, and control passes into the hands of the fiscal authorities.

Some final considerations
on economic philosophy

The foregoing conclusions merely express, in the monetary field, certain economic truths that are of a general nature because they are the direct consequence of the methods of influencing individual behavior.

Cash balances are supplied by purchasers and demanded by sellers in the market. If money was an ordinary form of wealth, equilibrium between demand and supply would be ensured by its price variation. But the price of money, because it is a standard of value, invariably is equal to one, and for that reason cannot vary.

However, this special feature of money does not prevent the adjustment mechanism from operating. It only modifies its appearance.

I have shown, in fact, that imbalance between supply of and demand for money generated an inverse imbalance between aggregate demand and aggregate supply of real wealth. This relation, by generating a shift in the general level of prices, generates in fact a variation in the price of money relative to the prices of other forms of wealth considered as a whole, and affects the demand for and supply of money, through variations in the cash balances necessary for the settlement of transactions. This is how the actual functioning of the adjustment mechanism inherent in all market phenomena can be depicted.

However, if one wants to guard against a shift in the general level of prices as the natural consequence of a difference between supply of and demand for money, there is only one way to act—namely, to influence directly the existing quantity of money by supplying the additional amounts desired or by reabsorbing the excess amounts which are undesired. It is this method of direct quantitative adjustment that is used the moment the market rate reaches the level of the discount rate. This accounts for the effectiveness of the instrument which control of the discount rate places in the hands of the monetary authorities, but it also accounts for its limitations.

Being the sluice gate which commands access to the reserves of the system of issue, the discount rate holds them back so long as it remains above the market rate, but passively allows them to flow out in response to the requirements of the latter the moment its level is reached or exceeded by the rate which, in the absence of any discount possibility, would secure market equilibrium.

Thus, the monetary authorities do not fix the amount of individual cash balances, but determine the way in which they are provided, at least so long as they are not practically unable to raise the platform giving access to their reserves to a level sufficient to protect them against the demands to which they are subjected.

AFTERWORD

Since writing this study, I have taken cognizance of a conclusive memorandum by M. Pierre Berger, Inspector of the Bank of France, dated January 18, 1957. The author shows with extreme precision that

> a fall or a rise in gold or foreign exchange holdings, in the assets of the Central Bank, is not passed on to the stock of money on hand, but generates variations inverse to the evolution of banking assets. In other words, when foreign exchange reserves or gold holdings decline, no contraction in the stock of money is noted, but only an increase in the amount of credit granted, and—inversely—when gold or foreign exchange reserves increase, one notes a decline in the amount of credit granted and not an increase in the volume of money. This phenomenon can be observed not only under the gold standard (nineteenth and early twentieth centuries), but also under a system of paper currency, whether or not associated with exchange controls (interwar experience and recent experience).

His analysis leads him to the conclusion that

> availabilities taken up by purchases of foreign exchange or generated by sales of foreign exchange tend to be reconstituted or to be reabsorbed—sometimes even immediately— to the extent that the behavior of money holders continues unchanged.

The whole memorandum can be regarded as bearing out the contention that the quantity of money in circulation is not an effect of the volume of assets as a counterpart to which it is issued, but the result of the aggregate level of the desired cash balances.